SWIRL, SIP & SAVOR

NORTHWEST WINE AND SMALL PLATE PAIRINGS

Carol Frieberg

with Andy Perdue

SASQUATCH BOOKS
SEATTLE

Printed in China

Published by Sasquatch Books

Distributed by PGW/Perseus

15 14 13 12 11 10   9 8 7 6 5 4 3 2 1

Cover photographs: Lara Ferroni

Cover design: Henry Quiroga

Interior design and composition: Henry Quiroga

Interior photographs: Lara Ferroni

Library of Congress Cataloging-in-Publication Data

Frieberg, Carol

Swirl, sip & savor : Northwest wine and small plate pairings / Carol Frieberg with Andy Perdue.

p. cm.

Includes index.

ISBN 978-1-57061-562-7

1. Appetizers--Northwest, Pacific. 2. Wine and wine making--Northwest, Pacific. I. Perdue, Andy. II. Title.

TX740.F677 2010

641.8'12--dc22

2009039984

Sasquatch Books

119 South Main Street, Suite 400

Seattle, WA 98104

(206) 467-4300

www.sasquatchbooks.com

custserv@sasquatchbooks.com

Contents

Foreword

Since the late 1990s, the wine regions of Washington, Oregon, British Columbia, and Idaho have matured well beyond anything but wild expectations. Perhaps 250 wineries dotted the landscape back then. But as of this writing, the Northwest wine industry is more than one thousand wineries strong.

What can wine do for a region? Eastern Washington has been transformed from vast, arid stretches into a romantic adventure. Until the late 1990s, Walla Walla was best known for its penitentiary. Today it is home to more than one hundred wineries and the amenities that come along with them. Wine has turned sleepy Yamhill County, southwest of Portland, into a home for more than one hundred wineries—all of which craft world-class Pinot Noir. Bed-and-breakfasts and restaurants cater to the lifestyle that comes with being in wine country. Wine has turned British Columbia's Okanagan Valley into the hottest wine region in Canada. More than a hundred wineries line the valley, along with restaurants, hotels, galleries, and more.

Wineries are changing the landscape of the Pacific Northwest. Today, enthusiasts can go wine touring across bucolic Vancouver Island, the Olympic Peninsula, Southern Oregon's Rogue and Umpqua valleys, as well as the length of Idaho—from the top of the Panhandle to the Nevada border. Wine has transformed the Pacific Northwest into one of the nation's great food regions and travel destinations. History is happening.

—ANDY PERDUE
2010

Introduction

"Like the yin and yang of a lasting marriage, great wine pairings bring out the best in each other."

—Rocco DiSpirito, chef and author of *Flavor*

As old definitions of marriage and relationships are changing, so too are the old rules which once applied to pairing food and wine. Guidelines are now more flexible and reflect the growing presence of complex and multi-ethnic flavors. The ultimate goal remains constant however; that food and wine be savored together, rather than consumed separately.

For anyone who loves good food, who appreciates fine wines, and who is interested in learning how they pair well together, here is a collection of innovative pairing suggestions from some of the finest wine producers in the Pacific Northwest. Here you will find appetizer and small plate recipes from winemakers, winegrowers, caterers and chefs. These folks have paired their favorite recipes with some of the finest wines available from the region. And not only do these recipes showcase the magnificent wines, they also highlight the abundance of local ingredients that we are so blessed with here in the Northwest—hazelnuts, artisan cheese, Dungeness crab, clams, mussels, oysters, organic meats, apples, pears, berries, honey, wild mushrooms, and of course, the grapes themselves.

Whether you are on a wine tasting weekend or simply stopping in at your local market for a bottle of wine, you now have the ideal resource from which to choose a recipe that will pair perfectly with your wine. There are many options to choose from—a dry Viognier paired with Molded Salmon Pâté (page 22), a creamy Pinot Gris paired with Blue Cheese and Hazelnut Crostini (page 34), or a fruity, peppery Syrah paired with grilled Herbed Lamb Chops with Syrah Reduction (page 128). A small plate feast awaits you, whether you're planning dinner for two or twenty-two.

While it's helpful to have suggestions from the experts, you can mix and match these recipes with complimentary wines. The only rule of thumb to follow is that a wine should complement the food rather than dominate it. Match the bigness of the wine with the bigness of the food—serve light food with light wine, and heavier food with heavier wine. Soups, salads, and light dishes are best when accompanied by light, crisp wines, while more robust foods like grilled steaks and chops prefer bigger, stronger wines.

Other than that, there are no strict rules to follow when pairing food and wine. Some people prefer matching like with like, pairing a citrusy wine with a citrusy sauce or a buttery wine with a buttery sauce. Others prefer to contrast flavors—pairing a spicy meat stew with a slightly sweet wine or a rich, creamy cheese with a bright, crisp wine. As in all relationships, there's no right or wrong combination. Some people are attracted to opposites, and some are drawn to those more like themselves. Discover the pairing that is perfect for you, and celebrate that union.

—CAROL FRIEBERG
2010

DIPS AND SPREADS

Fig and Olive Tapenade

Salt Spring Vineyards | Salt Spring Island, British Columbia

Makes about 2 cups

1 cup dried figs, stemmed

1¼ cups pitted kalamata olives

2 tablespoons capers, rinsed

2 teaspoons dried thyme leaves

2 teaspoons fresh rosemary, finely chopped

2 teaspoons minced garlic

Juice of 1 lemon (about 3 tablespoons)

¼ teaspoon salt

Freshly ground black pepper

⅓ cup extra virgin olive oil

In a food processor, blend the figs, olives, capers, thyme, rosemary, garlic, lemon juice, salt, pepper to taste, and olive oil to desired consistency.

Serve warm or at room temperature in a small bowl, surrounded with crackers or French bread.

....

WINE PAIRING: *Salt Spring Vineyards Blanc de Noir (Pinot Noir Rosé)*
This dry Provence-style Rosé offers lots of bright fresh berry and a hint of lemon zest. Think adult strawberry lemonade!

Hot Artichoke Crab Dip

Paradisos del Sol | Zillah, Washington

Makes about 2 cups

  1 cup mayonnaise

  1 cup finely grated Parmesan cheese

  One 6.5-ounce jar marinated artichoke hearts, rinsed, drained, and chopped

  6 ounces fresh cooked Dungeness crabmeat, finely chopped

  1 tablespoon minced garlic

Preheat the oven to 350 degrees F.

In a small bowl, mix together the mayonnaise, Parmesan, artichoke hearts, crabmeat, and garlic. Spoon the mixture into an oven-safe dish. Bake uncovered for 25 minutes, or until slightly brown.

Serve warm with crackers.

COOK'S NOTE: You may substitute canned crabmeat or imitation crabmeat for the Dungeness crabmeat.

RECIPE CONTRIBUTED BY TOBY ERICKSON

....

WINE PAIRING: *Paradisos del Sol Rosé Paradiso, Yakima Valley*
Barrel-fermented and barrel-aged Rosé, based on the Sangiovese grape, blends in Rosés made from Cabernet Sauvignon, Malbec, and Tempranillo for complexity and richness. This is more than a simple picnic wine—it is rich and round with a lovely bouquet.

Baked Spinach Artichoke Dip

Tucker Cellars Winery | Sunnyside, Washington

Makes about 1½ cups

> One 8-ounce package cream cheese, softened
>
> ½ cup grated Parmesan cheese
>
> ½ teaspoon crushed red pepper flakes
>
> ¼ teaspoon salt
>
> 1 clove garlic, crushed
>
> Dash freshly ground black pepper
>
> One 6.5-ounce jar marinated artichoke hearts, rinsed, drained, and chopped
>
> ½ cup frozen spinach, thawed and squeezed dry

Preheat the oven to 350 degrees F.

In a medium bowl, mix the cream cheese and Parmesan until well combined. Stir in the crushed red pepper flakes, salt, garlic, and pepper. Fold in the artichoke hearts and spinach. Transfer the mixture to a glass or ceramic baking dish. Bake uncovered for 30 to 35 minutes, until heated through.

Serve hot with crusty bread or crackers.

COOK'S NOTE: This recipe can be made a day ahead and refrigerated until time of baking.

....

WINE PAIRING: *Tucker Cellars Viognier*
A richly blended wine with flavors of pear, pineapple, and spices, and a hint of oak aging. Crisp and delightful to sip, this unique blend of Viognier, Pinot Gris, and Muscat Ottenel gives this off-dry wine a smooth finish.

Pesto Cream Cheese Spread

Robert Karl Cellars | Spokane, Washington

Makes about 3 cups

> ¼ cup coarsely chopped fresh basil
>
> 1 green onion, chopped
>
> 2 cloves garlic, chopped
>
> ¾ cup chopped pine nuts
>
> Two 8-ounce packages cream cheese, softened
>
> 1 cup grated Parmesan cheese
>
> ½ cup extra virgin olive oil

In a food processor, pulse the basil, green onion, and garlic until minced. Add the pine nuts, cream cheese, Parmesan, and olive oil. Blend the mixture until smooth. Refrigerate in an airtight container for at least 4 hours or overnight to meld the flavors.

Serve with crackers or toasted baguette slices.

....

WINE PAIRING: *Robert Karl Cellars Columbia Valley Claret*
The inviting aromas of cocoa-dusted black cherries, black currant, briar, and espresso unfold on the palate with flavors of chewy black cherry, plum, and a note of smoke on the finish.

Three-Cheese Fondue

Black Widow Winery | Penticton, British Columbia

Makes about 4½ cups

>   4 tablespoons butter
>
>   2 tablespoons minced garlic
>
>   2 cups light cream
>
>   2 tablespoons cornstarch
>
>   ¼ cup Black Widow Oasis or other white wine
>
>   4 ounces fontina cheese, cut into cubes (about 1 cup)
>
>   4 ounces provolone cheese, shredded (about 1 cup)
>
>   2 ounces Gorgonzola cheese, crumbled (about ½ cup)
>
>   1 cup fresh spinach, cut into chiffonade
>
>   ½ cup chopped sun-dried tomatoes
>
>   Freshly ground black pepper
>
>   Prepared olive tapenade (store-bought or homemade)

In a medium heavy saucepan, heat the butter over medium-low heat. Add the garlic and stir constantly for 2 minutes, or until golden.

Pour the light cream into a small bowl and whisk in the cornstarch. Add the light cream mixture to the saucepan and whisk for 3 minutes, or until it comes to a simmer (do not let boil). Pour in the white wine and continue simmering until slightly thickened, about 3 minutes. Reduce the heat to low and stir in the fontina, provolone, and Gorgonzola until smooth. Stir in the spinach, sun-dried tomatoes, and pepper to taste. Transfer the hot cheese mixture to a fondue pot and burner or a chafing dish. Place a dollop of the olive tapenade in the center of the fondue.

Serve immediately with dippers such as Asiago cheese bread cubes, blanched asparagus spears, and baby carrots.

COOK'S NOTE: To make spinach chiffonade, tightly roll the fresh spinach leaves, then cut them crosswise into thin strips using a sharp knife. The leaves form long, thin shreds when they are unrolled. This cheese fondue can be made in advance (before adding the spinach and sun-dried tomatoes), then carefully reheated over medium-low heat before completing the recipe.

RECIPE CONTRIBUTED BY MARY ANN WALLACE

....

WINE PAIRING: *Black Widow Oasis*
Fragrant and drinkable, this white wine blend is made from Gewürztraminer, Schönburger, and Pinot Gris grapes. The wine is crisp and complex, with an off-dry finish and abundant fruity bouquet.

Phyllo-Wrapped Brie

Paradise Ranch Wines | Vancouver, British Columbia

Makes 8 appetizer servings

  3 frozen phyllo sheets (from 1-pound box), thawed to room temperature

  Extra-virgin olive oil for brushing phyllo

  One 8-ounce round Brie (about 4 inches in diameter)

  ¼ cup preserves (cranberry, apricot, or fig) or prepared chutney

Preheat the oven to 350 degrees F.

To prevent the dough from drying out, cover with plastic wrap and a damp kitchen towel, while assembling. On a baking sheet, smooth out one sheet of the phyllo. Lightly brush it with olive oil. Cover the first sheet of phyllo with a second sheet at a slight angle, and lightly brush with olive oil. Repeat with a third sheet of phyllo, placing it at a slight angle. (This enables the formation of a complete circle of phyllo around the Brie.) Cut the round of Brie in half horizontally. Place the bottom half in the center of the layered phyllo sheets. Spoon the preserves evenly over the bottom half of the Brie. Top with the remaining half of the round. Wrap the Brie with the phyllo and lightly brush with olive oil. Place on the center rack in the oven and bake for 10 to 15 minutes.

Serve warm with French bread or crackers.

....

WINE PAIRING: *Paradise Ranch Pinot Blanc Late Harvest Wine*
This soft, full-bodied wine with flavors of honeydew melon, pear, and apricot finishes with the sweetness of honey. A little taste of paradise.

Crater Lake Blue Cheese Spread

Cliff Creek Cellars | Gold Hill, Oregon

Makes about 3 cups

> 1 cup crumbled Rogue Creamery Crater Lake Blue Cheese or other blue cheese (about 4 ounces)
>
> 4 ounces cream cheese, softened
>
> ½ cup chopped candied pecans or walnuts (store-bought or homemade)
>
> ½ cup chopped dried cranberries or dried chopped cherries

Mix the blue cheese and cream cheese in a medium bowl until well-combined. Stir in the pecans and cranberries until combined.

Serve at room temperature with crackers.

....

WINE PAIRING: *Cliff Creek Cellars Syrah*

This 100 percent estate-grown Syrah is rich and full-bodied, with flavors of black raspberry and a hint of smoke. The nose is full with the essence of dark chocolate and black cherry.

Q: What does "Reserve" stand for on a label?

A: Unlike in Europe, where the word "Reserve" is a legal term with very strict rules about quality and ageing, in the United States it has no legal meaning. Some American wineries may use it to designate a special bottling or limited production, but others simply use it for a marketing tool.

Smoked Salmon Spread

Scott Paul Wines | Carlton, Oregon

Makes about 1¼ cups

6 ounces smoked salmon, skin removed

2 ounces cream cheese, softened

2 tablespoons finely chopped shallot

1 tablespoon light cream

1 tablespoon fresh lemon juice

Freshly ground black pepper

Flake the salmon, using a fork, into a small bowl. Stir in the cream cheese, then incorporate the shallot, light cream, lemon juice, and pepper to taste. Adjust amounts for desired consistency and taste.

Serve on crackers or crostini.

. . . .

WINE PAIRING: *Scott Paul La Paulée Pinot Noir*
Swirling fruit and flower notes invite you for a closer look. The first impression on the palate is its rich and silky texture that is long and lingering. Ripe cherries, raspberry notes, and black fruit undertones develop and flow into a smooth finish.

Chèvre with Honey and Almonds
Vista Hills Vineyard | Dayton, Oregon

Makes about 1½ cups

> 8 ounces goat cheese (chèvre), softened
>
> 3 to 4 tablespoons lavender honey
>
> ¼ cup slivered almonds

Place the goat cheese in a serving bowl. Drizzle with honey to taste and sprinkle with almonds.

Serve with water crackers or baguette slices.

....

WINE PAIRING: *Vista Hills Treehouse Estate Pinot Gris*
This wine displays exotic tropical aromatics followed by bright fruit and a crisp finish. A light touch of residual sugar provides roundness and balance.

Cardwell Hill Cheese Ball

Cardwell Hill Cellars | Philomath, Oregon

Makes about 4 cups

> 1 cup crumbled blue cheese (about 4 ounces)
>
> 1½ cups grated Cheddar cheese (about 6 ounces)
>
> One 12-ounce tub cream cheese
>
> 1 tablespoon grated white onion
>
> 1 tablespoon fresh parsley, chopped
>
> ½ teaspoon Worcestershire sauce
>
> ¾ cup toasted nuts (walnuts, pecans, hazelnuts, or almonds), finely chopped
>
> ¼ cup Cardwell Hill Cellars Pinot Gris or other dry white wine

In a medium bowl, combine the blue cheese, Cheddar cheese, cream cheese, onion, parsley, Worcestershire sauce, ¼ cup of the nuts, and the wine. Mix well and, using your hands, shape the mixture into a ball. Put the ball back in the bowl, cover with plastic wrap, and refrigerate 4 hours or overnight.

Remove from the refrigerator about a half hour before serving. Roll the cheese ball in the remaining nuts. Place on a serving plate surrounded by a variety of crackers.

WINE PAIRING: *Cardwell Hill Cellars Pinot Gris*
This is a refreshing wine with flavors of apple and citrus, followed by minerality and a hint of sweet melon and honey in the soft finish.

Dukkah (Egyptian Spice Blend)

RockWall Cellars | Omak, Washington

Makes about 2 cups

  ⅔ cup raw almonds

  ⅔ cup blanched hazelnuts, skins removed

  ⅓ cup pine nuts

  ½ cup pistachio nuts

  2½ teaspoons ground coriander

  2 teaspoons ground cardamom

  2 teaspoons ground cumin

  1½ teaspoons fennel seed

  1 teaspoon dried thyme leaves

  ½ teaspoon garlic powder

  ½ teaspoon salt

  ¼ teaspoon freshly ground black pepper

  Extra-virgin olive oil for dipping

  Balsamic vinegar for dipping

Preheat the oven to 350 degrees F.

In a food processor, finely grind all dry ingredients. Spread the nut-spice mixture evenly on a baking sheet. Place on the center rack in the oven and roast for 10 minutes, stirring halfway through.

To serve, place the Dukkah, olive oil, and balsamic vinegar in three separate small dishes. Dip small pieces of warm artisan bread in the olive oil and balsamic vinegar, and then into the Dukkah.

WINE PAIRING: *RockWall Cellars Auxerrois*

Auxerrois is a slightly dry fruit-forward wine with hints of apricot, pear, and citrus. An elegant white wine with a pleasant light floral bouquet.

Q: What do the letters "MV" stand for on a wine label?

A: "MV" indicates that a wine has been blended from grapes harvested in two or more vintages. The label is often stamped with "MV" in the place where the vintage year would typically appear on the label.

Baba Ganoush (Eggplant Spread)

Brian Carter Cellars | Woodinville, Washington

Makes about 2½ cups

        1 large eggplant, halved lengthwise

        2 medium red bell peppers, halved and seeded, veins removed

        1 small red onion, cut into 1-inch-thick rings

        5 tablespoons extra virgin olive oil, divided

        3 cloves garlic, finely chopped

        2 teaspoons cumin seed, toasted and ground

        1 teaspoon coriander seed, toasted and ground

        ½ teaspoon ground cayenne pepper

        ½ bunch fresh cilantro, stemmed and coarsely chopped

        1 tablespoon red wine vinegar

        Juice of ½ lemon (about 1 to 2 tablespoons)

        Salt and freshly ground black pepper

Preheat the oven to 400 degrees F.

Place the eggplant, red bell peppers, and red onion on a baking sheet; coat with 2 tablespoons of the olive oil. Place on the center rack in the oven and roast until very soft, about 40 minutes.

When cool enough, peel the eggplant and red peppers (optional). Finely chop the eggplant, red peppers, and red onions and place them in a large mixing bowl. Stir in the garlic, cumin, coriander, cayenne pepper, and cilantro.

In a small bowl, whisk together the red wine vinegar, lemon juice, and the remaining olive oil. Toss with the roasted vegetable mixture. Season to taste with salt and pepper.

Serve with pita bread wedges.

WINE PAIRING: *Brian Carter Cellars Byzance*

Seductively balanced with well-integrated tannins and layers of black raspberry, dark fruit, and spice, this Southern Rhone-Style Blend offers wild raspberries, licorice, bay, and pepper spice aromas.

BRIAN CARTER CELLARS

You will never taste the first wine Brian Carter made. In fact, nobody ever did. That first batch was a blackberry wine he made as a young lad, and the fermenting juice exploded, leaving quite an impact on his mother's kitchen. Since then, Carter's skills have improved immensely. In fact, he has been one of Washington's most respected winemakers for a quarter of a century.

Carter made a name for himself at Paul Thomas Wines in the Yakima Valley, producing not only fruit wines but also award-winning Chardonnay. When that winery sold in the late 1980s, he moved to the new Washington Hills Cellars in Sunnyside. There he produced wines under the Washington Hills, Apex, and W. B. Bridgman labels, earning high honors and accolades while he oversaw a fast-growing operation known for great values and high-end wines.

As early as 1997, Carter was thinking about his eponymous label—and even produced a red blend from that vintage under the Brian Carter Cellars label. He got more serious in 2000 and began putting together a slew of wines—all blends. They reflect his artistry in the bottle (and some cool artwork on the label) as well as his expertise in acquiring some of the state's finest grapes. These blends are loosely modeled on the wines of Bordeaux, Tuscany, and Chateauneuf-du-Pape. Carter has come a long way since that fateful day in his mom's kitchen, and we're just now seeing the full extent of his genius.

Shiitake Tapenade with Pinot Noir Reduction

Rex Hill Vineyards | Newberg, Oregon

Makes about 1 cup

> 2 tablespoons butter
>
> 2 tablespoons Extra-virgin olive oil
>
> 1 medium sweet onion, finely chopped
>
> 2 cloves garlic, chopped
>
> 8 ounces fresh shiitake mushrooms, stemmed and finely chopped
>
> Salt and freshly ground black pepper
>
> 1 cup Rex Hill Reserve Pinot Noir or other dry red wine
>
> 2 tablespoons balsamic vinegar
>
> Pinot Noir Reduction (recipe follows)

Heat the butter and olive oil in a large saucepan over medium heat. Stir in the onions and garlic and cook until the onions are translucent, about 5 minutes. Stir in the mushrooms and continue cooking until they are tender, about 5 minutes. Season to taste with salt and pepper.

Pour in the red wine and balsamic vinegar. Continue cooking until most of the liquid has evaporated, about 8 to 10 minutes.

Serve warm or at room temperature in a small bowl, surrounded with crostini or crackers. Place the Pinot Noir Reduction in a small pitcher and drizzle over the tapenade as desired.

Pinot Noir Reduction

1 ½ cups Rex Hill Pinot Noir or other dry red wine

Heat the red wine in small saucepan over medium-high heat. Stir frequently, until the wine is reduced to a syrup, about 10 to 15 minutes.

COOK'S NOTE: The tapenade can be made ahead and refrigerated in an airtight container for up to two days before serving.

....

WINE PAIRING: *Rex Hill Reserve Pinot Noir*

This Pinot Noir was selected from individual small French oak barrels from premium Willamette Valley vineyards. It boasts flavors of black cherry, cola, and chocolate, with a nose of earth, spice, minerals, stone fruit, and sappy cherry.

> **Q:** How much alcohol does most table wine contain?
>
> **A:** Most wines are 8 to 14 percent alcohol. If wine exceeds 14 percent, the alcohol content must be displayed on the label.

Salmon Mousse
with Parsley and Chive Pesto

Edmonds Winery | Woodinville, Washington

Makes about 2 cups

    1 tablespoon butter

    1 tablespoon minced shallots

    1 pound salmon fillet, skin removed

    1 to 2 cups Edmonds Winery Sauvignon Blanc or other dry white wine

    1 bay leaf

    Buerre Blanc Sauce (recipe follows)

    Parsley and Chive Pesto (recipe follows)

In a nonstick skillet, melt the butter over medium heat. Add the shallots and cook, stirring until tender, about 3 minutes.

Put the salmon in the skillet and pour in the wine, enough to almost cover the salmon. Drop in the bay leaf. Reduce heat to medium-low. Cover and cook the salmon until the thickest part flakes with a knife, about 5 to 6 minutes. Remove the salmon from the poaching liquid and let cool slightly. Strain and reserve the poaching liquid (for making the Buerre Blanc Sauce).

To make the mousse, break the salmon into small pieces and blend in a food processor. Pulse until the salmon is roughly chopped. Slowly mix in the Buerre Blanc Sauce and process until the mixture is smooth. Transfer the mousse to a covered serving dish and refrigerate 4 hours or until firm.

To serve, top crostini or crackers with salmon mousse and drizzle lightly with parsley and chive pesto.

Buerre Blanc Sauce

 1 tablespoon butter

 2 tablespoon minced shallots

 1 cup reserved poaching liquid (from the salmon)

 1 cup Edmonds Winery Sauvignon Blanc or other dry white wine

 ½ cup heavy cream

In a small saucepan, melt the butter over medium heat. Add the shallots and cook, stirring until tender, about 3 minutes. Pour in the reserved poaching liquid and wine; simmer uncovered until the liquid is reduced to ¼ cup. Slowly stir in the heavy cream and simmer until the sauce thickens (it should adhere to the back of a spoon). Strain.

Parsley and Chive Pesto

 ½ cup coarsely chopped Italian parsley

 ½ cup coarsely chopped chives

 1 clove garlic, chopped

 1 tablespoon pine nuts

 ¼ teaspoon salt

 ½ cup extra virgin olive oil

Put the parsley, chives, garlic, pine nuts, and salt in a food processor. Pulse while slowly adding the olive oil until the pesto is smooth. Place in an airtight container in the refrigerator until ready to use.

....

WINE PAIRING: *Edmonds Winery Sauvignon Blanc*
This is 100 percent Sauvignon Blanc at its finest. Notes of pears, citrus, and a touch of grass are detected in this crisp, well-balanced wine. Serve with shellfish, salmon, halibut, and grilled chicken.

Molded Salmon Pâté

Devitt Winery | Jacksonville, Oregon

Makes about 4 cups

> 1 pound poached salmon fillet, flaked (or one 16-ounce can salmon, drained and flaked)
>
> ½ cup finely chopped red onion
>
> ½ cup finely chopped pitted kalamata olives
>
> ½ cup capers, drained and rinsed
>
> Two ¼-ounce envelopes unflavored gelatin
>
> ½ cup cold water
>
> 1⅔ cups mayonnaise
>
> 1 to 2 ripe avocados, thinly sliced and sprinkled with fresh lemon juice
>
> Dill Sauce (recipe follows)

In a medium bowl, mix together the salmon, red onion, olives, and capers.

In a small microwave-safe glass bowl, sprinkle the gelatin on the cold water. Let it stand for a few minutes. Microwave the mixture on high for 1 to 1½ minutes, stirring until clear. Let mixture cool for 5 minutes.

In a large bowl, mix together the mayonnaise and gelatin until smooth. Fold in the salmon mixture until completely combined. Put half of the salmon pâté in a greased 4- by 8-inch loaf pan (or a 4-cup mold) and top with the avocado slices. Cover with the remaining pâté. Cover with plastic wrap and refrigerate for at least 4 hours or overnight.

To unmold the pâté, place the loaf pan in hot water (just enough to cover sides) for 30 to 60 seconds, then invert onto a serving dish. Just before serving, spoon the Dill Sauce over the pâté. If desired, sprinkle with fresh dill or top with additional avocado slices.

Serve with crackers.

Dill Sauce

2 cups sour cream

2 tablespoons Dijon mustard

2 tablespoons fresh lemon juice

2 tablespoons chopped fresh dill, or 2 teaspoons dried dill

In a medium bowl, whisk together the sour cream, mustard, lemon juice, and dill. Refrigerate in an airtight container until ready to use.

. . . .

WINE PAIRING: *Devitt Viognier, Applegate Valley*

Completely dry, with an aromatic nose of peaches, apricots, and pineapple notes, this wine has a great mouthfeel and long finish.

Q: If an American wine is labeled with the name of a grape such as Chardonnay, what is the minimum percentage of that grape that must be used?

A: In Washington it is 75 percent and in Oregon it is 90 percent (except for Cabernet, which can be 75 percent).

Egg and Caviar Pie

Long Shadows Vintners | Walla Walla, Washington

Makes 12 appetizer servings

>   6 hard-cooked eggs, peeled and chopped
>
>   6 tablespoons butter, softened
>
>   1 tablespoon mayonnaise
>
>   1 ½ cups chopped scallions
>
>   One 8-ounce package cream cheese, softened
>
>   3 ½ to 4 ounces good-quality caviar

Grease an 8-inch springform pan. In a medium bowl, mix together the eggs, butter, and mayonnaise until well combined, then spread the mixture evenly in the pan. Sprinkle with scallions. Using a wet spatula, gently spread the cream cheese over the scallions until smooth. Cover with plastic wrap and refrigerate for 3 hours or overnight.

Before serving, top with caviar and spread it to the pan's edges. Run a knife around the sides to loosen the pie and remove the springform. Garnish with lemon wedges and parsley sprigs if desired.

Serve with small toasts or crackers.

....

WINE PAIRING: *Long Shadows Vintners Poet's Leap Riesling*
Bright and balanced, this clean and refreshing wine has aromas and flavors showcasing the purity of the grape. White peaches, honey, a pleasing mineral note, and a hint of ripe apricot are enhanced by the wine's crisp acidity and fresh, lively finish.

LONG SHADOWS VINTNERS

Back in the 1990s, Allen Shoup had the idea of creating a collaboration that could put Washington Riesling on the international stage. At the time he was CEO of Stimson Lane (now Ste. Michelle Wine Estates) and was, for all intents and purposes, the most powerful figure in the Washington wine industry. The resulting projects were Col Solare, a red wine with the Antinori family of Tuscany, and Eroica, a Riesling with Ernst Loosen of Germany. They were (and remain) hugely popular and highly sought-after wines.

When Shoup retired from Ste. Michelle in 2001, he never thought of leaving the wine industry. In fact, those international collaborations were central in his mind. Thus he launched Long Shadows, a group of seven wineries. Each is headed by Shoup, who brings in a "celebrity" winemaker/partner from internationally known wine regions, including Napa, Bordeaux, Tuscany, and Australia. Behind the scenes is Gilles Nicault, a Frenchman who serves as resident winemaker for the seven brands, taking care of the wines year-round and consulting with each international winemaker.

No doubt with Eroica in mind, Shoup created Poet's Leap, a Riesling produced by Armin Diel, one of Germany's most respected winemakers. It has been an instant hit, and the bottles are quickly gobbled up by an adoring and near-cult following.

FINGER FOODS

Deli Ham Roll-ups

White Bean, Tomato,
and Olive Bruschetta

Goat Cheese and Pesto
Crostini

Crostini with Caramelized
Walla Walla Sweet Onions

Blue Cheese and Hazelnut
Crostini

Spicy Tuna Tartar
on Rice Crackers

Sage Shortbread Crackers

Truffle Popcorn with Thyme
and Salt

Stilted Salmon on Crackers

Endive with Roquefort
and Balsamic Drizzle

Parmesan Wafers
with Prosciutto

Gorgonzola-Stuffed Figs

Eggplant Roll-ups

Chèvre and Mango Steak Spirals

Prosciutto-Wrapped Pear Bites

Quail Mousse Canapés

Flank Steak and Cambozola
Bites

Deli Ham Roll-ups

Patit Creek Cellars | Walla Walla, Washington

Makes 40 appetizer servings

> One 8-ounce tub whipped cream cheese
>
> 1 tablespoon Worcestershire sauce
>
> ¼ teaspoon garlic salt
>
> Two 10-ounce packages sliced ham (about 20 slices), cut in half
>
> One 16-ounce jar peperoncinis, drained, stemmed, and seeded (or one 10-ounce jar pickled white or green asparagus, drained and cut in half)

In a small mixing bowl, combine the cream cheese, Worcestershire sauce, and garlic salt. Lay the ham slices on a flat surface. Spread 1 teaspoon of the cream cheese mixture on each ham slice. Place the peperoncini or asparagus at one end of the ham slice and roll up. Secure with a toothpick. Repeat process with the remaining ham and cream cheese mixture.

Refrigerate for at least 2 hours before serving.

....

WINE PAIRING: *Patit Creek Cellars Cabernet Sauvignon*
This cabernet is soft, balanced, and polished, with red currant and black cherry flavors. Earthy and light coffee characteristics give way to a hint of chocolate at the finish.

White Bean, Tomato, and Olive Bruschetta

The Four Graces | Dundee, Oregon

Makes 24 appetizer servings

    1 artisan baguette, cut on the diagonal into 24 slices (about ½-inch thick)

    1½ cups canned Great Northern beans, rinsed and drained

    3 plum tomatoes, seeded and chopped

    ¼ cup chopped pitted kalamata olives

    ¼ cup chopped fresh basil

    1 tablespoon minced garlic

    6 tablespoons extra virgin olive oil, divided

    Salt and freshly ground black pepper

    6 ounces soft goat cheese (chèvre), room temperature

Preheat the broiler.

Place the baguette slices on a baking sheet and brush with 2 tablespoons of the olive oil. Broil until golden, about 1 to 2 minutes.

In a medium bowl, mix together the beans, tomatoes, olives, basil, garlic, and the remaining olive oil. Season to taste with salt and pepper.

Spread goat cheese on the baguette slices and top with the bean-tomato-olive mixture.

....

WINE PAIRING: *The Four Graces Dundee Hills Pinot Gris*
This wine is deliciously bright, fresh, and crisp, with an interesting minerality and acidity. Nectarine, pear, and melon notes combine with fresh meringue and Meyer lemon zest to lay the foundation for a lovely texture and crisp yet silky mouthfeel. Soft floral aromas of white rose petal and apple blossom.

Bon Appétit!
Mona Nutt
Et Fille Wines

Goat Cheese and Pesto Crostini

Et Fille Wines | Newberg, Oregon

Makes 24 appetizer servings

    1 artisan baguette, cut on the diagonal into 24 slices (about ½-inch thick)

    ¾ cup basil pesto (homemade or store-bought)

    8 ounces soft goat cheese (chèvre)

    6 small ripe Roma tomatoes, cut into ¼-inch slices (or 12 cherry tomatoes, halved)

Preheat the oven to 400 degrees F.

Put the baguette slices on a baking sheet and lightly toast both sides in the oven, approximately 3 minutes on each side. Remove from the oven and spread about 1 teaspoon of pesto on each slice. Spread gently with goat cheese and top with a slice of tomato. Bake for 5 to 7 minutes on the center rack in the oven.

Serve at room temperature.

....

WINE PAIRING: *Et Fille Pinot Noir, Kalita Vineyards*
A fresh, juicy, and approachable Pinot Noir, the Kalita has black cherry and mocha flavors that linger on the finish. Cola and herbs form both a complex nose and palette.

> **Q:** What is fortified wine?
>
> **A:** Wine that has the addition of alcohol to it, such as Port, Sherry, or Madeira. These wines are generally between 17 and 22 percent alcohol.

Crostini with Caramelized Walla Walla Sweet Onions

Trio Vintners | Walla Walla, Washington

Makes 20 appetizer servings

    1 artisan baguette, cut on the diagonal into 20 slices (about ½-inch thick)
    3 medium Walla Walla sweet onions
    2 tablespoons butter
    ¼ cup dry vermouth
    ½ tablespoon brown sugar
    ¼ teaspoon dried thyme leaves (or ¾ teaspoon chopped fresh thyme leaves)
    ¾ teaspoon salt
    ¼ teaspoon freshly ground black pepper
    2 tablespoons white balsamic vinegar or dark balsamic vinegar

Preheat the oven to 350 degrees F.

Place the baguette slices on a baking sheet and toast lightly in the oven, about 4 minutes on each side. Set aside.

Cut the onions lengthwise and place cut sides down, then cut crossways very thinly to make half circles. Cut these slices in half.

Melt the butter over medium heat in a 12-inch cast-iron skillet. Add the onions, stirring occasionally, until they start to caramelize, about 30 minutes. Mix in the vermouth, brown sugar, thyme, salt, and pepper. Continue cooking for 20 minutes, stirring occasionally, until the onions have thickened and the liquid has evaporated. Add the balsamic vinegar. Simmer uncovered for 10 to 15 minutes, or until the onions are golden brown and the liquid has evaporated.

To serve, pile the caramelized onions on the crostini. Sprinkle with a small amount of crumbled Gorgonzola cheese if desired.

WINE PAIRING: *Trio Vintners Lewis Vineyard Riesling*

This off-dry style wine boasts lovely aromas of peaches and cream and lychee nut. It presents a big mouthfeel while delivering refreshing acidity.

Q: Which wines need aerating, and for how long should they "breathe"?

A: The younger and more tannic the wine, the more time it needs to breathe. As a general rule, young tannic red wines soften up with 30 to 60 minutes of aeration. Lighter-bodied red wines (Pinot Noir, for example) that have lower tannin levels need little if any time to breathe.

Blue Cheese and Hazelnut Crostini

RoxyAnn Winery | Medford, Oregon

Makes 12 crostini

> 1 artisan baguette, cut on the diagonal into 12 slices (about ⅓ inch thick)
>
> 3 ounces Rogue Creamery blue cheese or other blue cheese
>
> ⅓ cup toasted hazelnuts, husks removed and coarsely chopped
>
> Wildflower honey for drizzling

Preheat the oven to 400 degrees F.

Place the baguette slices in a single layer on a baking sheet. Toast in the oven until golden, about 4 minutes on each side.

Spread the blue cheese on the crostini. Sprinkle with the hazelnuts and drizzle with honey.

COOK'S NOTE: The toasted baguette slices can be made ahead. Store in an airtight container for up to two days.

....

WINE PAIRING: *RoxyAnn Pinot Gris*
This brilliant straw-colored Pinot Gris has a creamy, balanced mouthfeel with bright citrus acidity and some enticing mineral notes in the finish. It offers floral notes, aromas of ripe pears, peach, and grapefruit with bright accents of tangerine, mango, and honeysuckle.

ROXYANN WINERY

For more than a hundred years, Hillcrest Orchard has been bearing fruit in the southern Oregon city of Medford. With this agricultural history in mind, Roxy-Ann Winery was launched in 2001. It was named after Roxy Ann Peak, a two-thousand-foot dormant volcano that rises above the Rogue Valley. The vineyard is on the slopes of Roxy Ann Peak and is planted with such warm-climate grapes as Cabernet Sauvignon, Cabernet Franc, Temprañillo, Grenache, Malbec, and Syrah.

In 2002 a young winemaker named Gus Janeway showed up at RoxyAnn to use the equipment for his own small label, Velocity Cellars. He was thrilled to be working alongside Sarah Powell, a longtime Northwest winemaker who was part-owner of RoxyAnn. In 2003, Powell, then forty-one, became ill and died a year later from cancer. The owners of RoxyAnn approached Janeway about staying on and crafting RoxyAnn's wines along-side those of his own Velocity. He agreed and was RoxyAnn's head wine-maker through 2008, when John Quinones took over. Quinones is a veteran winemaker from California who continues the tradition of crafting beautifully balanced wines that show off clarity of fruit and pair well with a variety of foods.

Those traits surely show up in RoxyAnn's wines, which lean heavily toward reds. Its releases include a Bordeaux-style blend called simply "Claret," as well as such varietals as Syrah, Merlot, Pinot Gris, and Viognier. The tasting room is in a charming converted stable and should be on anyone's list of stops while touring Southern Oregon's Rogue Valley.

Spicy Tuna Tartar on Rice Crackers

William Church Winery | Woodinville, Washington

Makes 8 appetizer servings

> 1 sushi-grade ahi tuna steak (12 ounces), cut into 1-inch pieces
>
> 1 Roma tomato, seeded and finely chopped
>
> ½ tablespoon fresh lime juice
>
> 2½ teaspoons extra virgin olive oil
>
> 2 teaspoons finely chopped fresh Thai basil
>
> 2 teaspoons finely chopped fresh cilantro
>
> 1 teaspoon toasted sesame seeds
>
> ¾ teaspoon hot pepper sauce
>
> One ¼-inch piece fresh ginger, peeled and finely chopped (about ½ teaspoon)
>
> Salt and freshly ground black pepper
>
> 40 sesame rice crackers

Pulse the ahi tuna in food processor several times, making sure some chunks remain. Transfer to a medium bowl and stir in the tomato, lime juice, olive oil, Thai basil, cilantro, sesame seeds, hot pepper sauce, ginger, and salt and pepper to taste.

Serve with rice crackers on a serving platter. Mound some tuna tartar in the center of each cracker and garnish with additional toasted sesame seeds if desired.

RECIPE CONTRIBUTED BY MARCUS RAFANELLI

....

WINE PAIRING: *William Church Viognier*

This wine bears flavors of stone fruit and fresh pear with honeysuckle floral notes. It's luscious, pale straw in color, and pairs well with seafood and spicy dishes.

Sage Shortbread Crackers

DiStefano Winery | Woodinville, Washington

Makes 10 dozen crackers

> 4 cups all-purpose flour
>
> ¾ pound (3 sticks) butter, softened
>
> 4 ounces cream cheese, softened
>
> 1 cup cold water
>
> 1 ½ teaspoons salt
>
> 1 ½ teaspoons coarsely ground black pepper
>
> ⅓ cup chopped fresh sage

Put the flour, butter, and cream cheese in a large mixing bowl. Using an electric mixer, blend on low until the butter and cream cheese are incorporated. (The mixture will still be quite dry.) Add the water, salt, pepper, and sage, and mix on low until a stiff dough is formed.

Remove the dough from the mixing bowl. Working on parchment or wax paper, cut the dough into three or four equal pieces and roll into logs about 1½ inches in diameter. Wrap each log in plastic wrap. Freeze overnight (or up to a month).

Remove the dough rolls from the freezer and allow them to thaw for 45 to 60 minutes before using.

Preheat the oven to 350 degrees F.

Cut the rolls into coins about ¼-inch thick. Place the coins on a lightly greased baking sheet about ¾-inch apart. Bake on the center rack in the oven for 15 to 18 minutes, or until light brown. Cool the crackers.

COOK'S NOTE: Rosemary or savory may also be used in this recipe. Or increase the amount of pepper in place of the herbs to make black pepper crackers.

RECIPE CONTRIBUTED BY EXECUTIVE CHEF GEORGE B. STEVENSON

WINE PAIRING: *DiStefano Meritage*

Notes of blackberries, black cherries, raspberries, and cassis mingle with dense notes of chocolate, cedar, and vanilla. A hint of toasted almonds and dried prunes are layered with traces of cracked pepper and spice. Berries and dried fruits linger on a full palate with ripe, chewy tannins and a long, creamy finish.

DISTEFANO WINERY

Perhaps only in Washington would a nuclear engineer become a winemaker. Although many of Washington's vineyards lie within modest driving distance from the Hanford Nuclear Reservation, this had no impact on Mark Newton's decision to turn to winemaking. Rather, it was a 1983 visit to Domaine Chandon. After tasting the famous Napa Valley winery's sparkling wine, he signed up for winemaking classes at the University of California at Davis. Within a year, he would launch Newton & Newton Winery using Oregon grapes. Success followed, as did a lawsuit from a similarly named winery in California, which forced Newton to change the winery's name.

Ultimately, he dropped the bubbly and now focuses on crafting great Cabernet Sauvignon, Merlot, Sauvignon Blanc, and Sémillon, along with a few others. In recent years, Newton has added Rhone varieties to his lineup and now makes some of Washington's finest Syrah and Viognier.

In recent years DiStefano has revamped its tasting room and added a dining facility in the barrel room, which offers a delicious four-course dinner for groups of up to twenty-six. Dining amid the barrels with friends is a unique wine country experience. Newton's small winery on the outskirts of Woodinville, Washington, tends to be overshadowed by more famous neighbors, but his wines are rarely outshone. In 2008, DiStefano earned the title Washington Winery of the Year by *Wine Press Northwest*. Not bad for a former nuclear engineer.

Truffle Popcorn with Thyme and Salt

Sumac Ridge Estate Winery | Summerland, British Columbia

Makes about 4 cups

> ⅓ cup popcorn kernels
>
> 4 teaspoons butter, melted
>
> 2 teaspoons white truffle oil
>
> 2 teaspoons chopped fresh thyme
>
> Truffle salt or sea salt

Pop the kernels in a hot-air popper. Toss in a large bowl with the butter, white truffle oil, and thyme. Season to taste with salt. Best served warm.

....

WINE PAIRING: *Sumac Ridge Steller's Jay Brut*

Ripe strawberries, fresh toast, and a crisp lively acidity are showcased in this exceptional sparkling wine. A hint of Pinot Noir blended with Chardonnay and Pinot Blanc gives it a fantastic copper color.

Q: What is the proper temperature to serve wine?

A: Red wine is best served between 58 and 65 degrees F. (Chilling in the refrigerator for about 15 minutes helps reach the correct temperature.) White wine is ideally served between 48 and 55 degrees F. (Some say the cheaper the wine, the cooler it should be served.)

Stilted Salmon on Crackers

Dry Falls Cellars | Moses Lake, Washington

Makes 12 appetizer servings

> 6 ounces White Stilton cheese with apricots or lemon peel
>
> Multigrain crackers
>
> 4 ounces smoked salmon, skin removed and flaked

In a microwave-safe glass dish, soften the cheese on defrost for approximately 30 seconds. Spread the cheese on the multigrain crackers and top with the smoked salmon.

RECIPE CONTRIBUTED BY DOROTHY DEHART

....

WINE PAIRING: *Dry Falls Cellars Wahluke Slope*
Green apple is the dominant flavor in this pure varietal with a crisp, clean finish. Lush aromas of pear, peach, and apricot are delicately expressed. Enjoy with appetizers of cheese, nuts, fruit, or paired with Pacific salmon or halibut.

Endive with Roquefort and Balsamic Drizzle

Canyon's Edge Winery | Mabton, Washington

Makes 12 appetizer servings

> 1/4 cup balsamic vinegar
>
> 1/2 teaspoon sugar
>
> 2 ounces Roquefort cheese, crumbled
>
> 1 large or 2 small anchovies, mashed (or 1 teaspoon anchovy paste)
>
> 1 Belgium endive, root trimmed and separated into leaves

To make the balsamic drizzle, heat the balsamic vinegar and sugar in a small saucepan over medium heat. Stir occasionally until reduced by half, about 5 minutes. Remove from heat and let cool.

In a small bowl, mash the Roquefort with the anchovy until well combined. On a flat surface, roll about a teaspoon of the cheese-anchovy mixture to form a small ball; repeat with the remaining mixture. Place the endive leaves on a large platter. Place the Roquefort-anchovy balls in the center of each endive leaf. Just before serving, drizzle with the balsamic reduction.

....

WINE PAIRING: *Canyon's Edge Cabernet Sauvignon Reserve*
Elegant soft tannins with a hint of ripe berry and coconut make this serious wine a delight to drink. This classic Northwest cabernet boasts toasty oak aromas with a hint of vanilla.

Parmesan Wafers with Prosciutto

Terra Blanca Winery and Estate Vineyard | Benton City, Washington

Makes 20 wafers

> 6 ounces coarsely grated Parmigiano-Reggiano cheese (about 1¼ cup)
>
> 4 ounces prosciutto (about 8 thin slices)

Heat a large nonstick pan over medium to medium-low heat. Sprinkle the Parmigiano-Reggiano into thin circles, about 2½ inches in diameter. (Do not layer too thickly—there should be gaps and holes.) Let the cheese melt and bubble until the tops of the rounds begin to turn golden, about 9 to 10 minutes (this may take less time after the first batch). The wafers should have some small lacy holes.

Remove the pan from heat and let cool 1 to 2 minutes. Using a nonstick spatula, gently lift the wafers from the pan and place on a paper towel to drain and crisp. You may have to experiment with the first few wafers to perfect the technique.

To serve, top each Parmesan wafer with a small piece of prosciutto. Serve at room temperature.

RECIPE CONTRIBUTED BY STEVE ARAKI

....

WINE PAIRING: *Terra Blanca Sauvignon Blanc, Yakima Valley*
This food-friendly wine exhibits lovely concentrated citrus flavors, dominated by ripe grapefruit and hints of lemon, melon, and tropical fruit. A firm backbone of bright acidity balances the fresh fruit flavors.

TERRA BLANCA WINERY
AND ESTATE VINEYARD

Keith Pilgrim has the perfect ingredients for success. His eighty-acre vineyard on venerable Red Mountain is next to vaunted Klipsun Vineyards. He bored caves deep into the soil to age his wines in perfect cellar conditions. And he has built the most magnificent winery in Washington. The wines are really good, too.

Pilgrim began working on his operation in the early 1990s and was ready to open to the public by 1997. As he waited for his estate vineyards to mature, he used grapes from other vineyards with solid results. Now that Pilgrim has greater control over his estate fruit, the wines are coming into their own. Terra Blanca produces a wide variety of wines and is gaining the most attention for its Syrahs, as well as a Bordeaux-style blend called Onyx. Dessert wines, including ice wines and a port, should not be overlooked.

In 2006 he completed construction of his new facility, a stunning Tuscan-style building with a giant tasting room, banquet facilities, and gorgeous vistas of the Yakima Valley. A summer afternoon spent sipping wine at Terra Blanca is just about as perfect as they come. It doesn't take long to forget you're in Eastern Washington and think about being in Napa or Tuscany. A visit to Terra Blanca provides a hint of where the Washington wine industry can go in terms of quality and hospitality. A tour is highly recommended, as it includes the winery, the caves, and tastes of Terra Blanca's entire lineup of wines.

rgonzola-Stuffed Figs

nderlea Vineyard and Winery | Dundee, Oregon

Makes 12 appetizer servings

> 12 ripe figs, stemmed
>
> ½ pound Gorgonzola cheese, cut into 12 small pieces
>
> 12 shelled walnut halves

Gently cut three-quarters of the way through each fig. Stuff with a chunk of Gorgonzola cheese and a walnut half.

Arrange the stuffed figs on a serving platter scattered with additional walnuts, sliced figs, and Gorgonzola to nibble on.

. . . .

WINE PAIRING: *Winderlea "ANA" Pinot Noir*
Classic garnet in color with cherry, strawberry, and cranberry aromas, this wine has great mouthfeel with layers of berries, spice, and a hint of earthiness in the finish.

Q: What are Meritage wines?

A: Red Meritage wines contain a blend of at least two of the following grapes: Cabernet Sauvignon, Cabernet Franc, Merlot, Malbec, and Petit Verdot—the classic Bordeaux grape varieties. White Meritage, which is far less common, must contain only Sauvignon Blanc and Sémillon.

Eggplant Roll-ups

Springhouse Cellar | Hood River, Oregon

Makes 15 appetizer servings

  2 tablespoons extra virgin olive oil

  2 tablespoons balsamic vinegar

  2 tablespoons soy sauce

  ½ teaspoon dried basil

  ½ teaspoon dried tarragon

  ¼ teaspoon dried thyme leaves

  ¼ teaspoon chopped fresh rosemary

  1 medium eggplant, cut into ⅜-inch slices

  15 medium stalks of asparagus

  4 ounces soft goat cheese (chèvre)

Preheat the oven to 450 degrees F.

In a small bowl, whisk together the olive oil, balsamic vinegar, soy sauce, basil, tarragon, thyme, and rosemary. Dip the eggplant slices in this mixture, then arrange the eggplant slices on a baking sheet. Bake uncovered for 10 minutes, then broil for 2 minutes (until the eggplant is cooked just enough to bend easily). Remove from the oven and let cool. Meanwhile, steam the asparagus for 3 minutes, then plunge into ice water. Remove and pat dry with a paper towel. Cut the asparagus so they are about 1 inch longer than the eggplant slices.

Spread the goat cheese on top of each eggplant slice (chèvre is easier to spread if you microwave it on defrost for 1 minute). Place one asparagus piece on one end of an eggplant slice, then roll up. Secure with toothpick. Serve at room temperature.

WINE PAIRING: *Springhouse Cellar Columbia Valley Cabernet Sauvignon*
This friendly wine is dense, rich, and intense harvested with perfect balance, red fruit aromatics, and a little American oak and cedar overtones.

Q: Why should I swirl my wine in my glass before drinking it?

A: By swirling your wine, oxygen is invited into the glass, which allows the aromas to escape.

Chèvre and Mango Steak Spirals

Bounty Cellars | Kelowna, British Columbia

Makes 30 appetizer servings

  1 flank steak (about 1 ½ to 1 ¾ pounds), trimmed, rinsed, and patted dry

  1 tablespoon extra virgin olive oil

  Salt and freshly ground black pepper

  1 tablespoon milk (plus more if needed)

  4 ounces soft goat cheese (chèvre)

  30 fresh small mint leaves

  15 dried mango pieces, cut into ¼- by 1-inch slices

Preheat a gas grill or light charcoal in a barbecue.

Lightly brush the grill rack or barbecue grate with oil. Rub the steak with the olive oil, and sprinkle liberally with salt and pepper. Place the steak on a rack over high heat or over a solid bed of very hot coals. Cook for 8 to 10 minutes, turning once, until the meat is firm when pressed on the thin end and quite pink inside (slice the steak to check). Transfer the steak to a plate and let cool at least 30 minutes.

To make cutting easier, put the steak in the freezer for 45 minutes. Using a very sharp knife, cut the steak across the grain on a cutting board, as thinly as possible. Reserve rendered meat juices in a small bowl and add enough milk to make 2 tablespoons of liquid. Add the goat cheese and mash to form a smooth paste.

Working with one strip at a time, lay the steak on a work surface. (Blot with a paper towel if wet.) Spread steak strips evenly with a scant teaspoon of the goat cheese mixture. Lay a mint leaf and mango sliver on one end of the steak strip, positioning them so that they stick out of one side of the meat. Roll up the steak strip starting at the end with the mint and mango. Place cut side

down on a serving platter with the mint leaf and mango slice standing up. Let stand 10 to 15 minutes at room temperature before serving.

....

WINE PAIRING: *Bounty Cellars Meritage*

This Meritage was crafted in the quintessential Bordeaux style of blending 50 percent Merlot with 25 percent Cabernet Sauvignon and 25 percent Cabernet Franc. The Cabernet Sauvignon brings notes of dark black currants along with rich dark chocolate, a tannin backbone that supports the warm nutmeg, clove spices, and earthiness of the Merlot. The Cabernet Franc adds subtle fresh raspberry notes and soft acidity.

Q: Why are some wines decanted?

A: Young red wines are decanted to soften their tannins and allow the bouquet to develop. Older red wines (eight to ten years or more) are decanted to remove any sediment that may have accumulated.

Prosciutto-Wrapped Pear Bites

See Ya Later Ranch | Okanagan Falls, British Columbia

Makes 16 appetizer servings

> 2 pears, peeled, cored, and halved
>
> 2 cups See Ya Later Riesling or other white wine
>
> ¼ cup orange juice
>
> 3 tablespoons sugar
>
> 21 fresh basil leaves, divided
>
> 8 ounces prosciutto (about 16 thin slices)
>
> 4 ounces soft goat cheese (chèvre), softened

To poach the pears, heat the pears, wine, orange juice, sugar, and five of the basil leaves in a small saucepan over medium heat. Simmer for 15 minutes, or until a knife can easily pierce the pears. Remove the pears from the liquid and let cool slightly before cutting the halves into four pieces each.

Lay the prosciutto slices on a flat surface and spread chèvre on each strip. Top with the remaining basil leaves and pieces of pear, then roll up.

....

WINE PAIRING: *See Ya Later Ranch Riesling*

Subtle floral aromas rise from the glass while fresh green apple and a **hint** of pineapple express fresh acidity. Crisp orchard fruits are balanced by notes of honey and melon for a clean, bright finish.

Quail Mousse Canapés

Wheatridge in the Nook Winery | Arlington, Oregon

Makes 24 appetizer servings

> 4 boneless and skinless quail breasts (or chukar or pheasant)
>
> 1 cup water
>
> ½ teaspoon dried tarragon
>
> 1 chicken bouillon cube
>
> One 3-ounce package cream cheese, softened
>
> ¼ cup sour cream (plus more if needed)
>
> 2 tablespoons sun-dried tomatoes in oil, drained and finely chopped
>
> Salt and freshly ground black pepper
>
> 1 English cucumber, cut into ¼-inch-thick slices

Place the quail breasts, water, tarragon, and chicken bouillon cube in a medium saucepan over medium heat. Cover and cook the quail until tender, 12 to 15 minutes. Drain and set aside to cool.

Coarsely chop the poached quail. In a food processor, combine the quail, cream cheese, sour cream, and sun-dried tomatoes until smooth and of piping consistency (add more sour cream if necessary to thin the mixture). Season to taste with salt and pepper.

Using a pastry bag with a rosette tip, pipe rosettes of the quail mixture onto the cucumber rounds (or dollop, using a spoon). If desired, garnish with sun-dried tomato slices and flat-leaf parsley.

RECIPE CONTRIBUTED BY CHEF SHERYL M. MASHOS

....

WINE PAIRING: *Wheatridge in the Nook Chardonnay*
Crispness on the palate comes alive with green apple and nutty essences. This balanced, complex wine has a long, clean finish.

Flank Steak and Cambozola Bites

Pondera Winery | Kirkland, Washington

Makes 40 appetizer servings

> 2 ounces Cambozola or mild blue cheese (about ½ cup)
>
> 1 flank steak (about 1½ pounds), trimmed, rinsed, and patted dry
>
> Salt and freshly ground black pepper
>
> 1 tablespoon heavy cream

Remove Cambozola cheese from the refrigerator 30 minutes before preparing.

Preheat a gas grill to medium heat.

Brush the grate lightly with oil. Sprinkle the flank steak with salt and pepper. Grill steak to desired doneness (about 6 minutes per side for medium rare; 7 minutes per side for medium).

Remove the steak from the grill and let it rest 8 to 10 minutes. Using a sharp knife, cut the steak as thinly as possible (⅛- to ¼-inch-thick slices), across the grain and on the bias. Slices from the center of the steak can be cut in half. Reserve rendered meat juices and set aside.

In a small bowl, using a fork, mash together the Cambozola and the reserved meat juices. Stir in the heavy cream until consistency of a thick paste is reached. Spread a thin layer of the cheese mixture on one side of each steak slice; roll the slices up and secure them with a toothpick. Serve these bites at room temperature.

....

WINE PAIRING: *Pondera Consensio*
The core of this wine is Stillwater Creek Cabernet, known for its low-yielding concentrated fruit. Black fruits like cassis and black cherry contain hints of cedar, mocha, and butterscotch along with some nice minerality.

HOT APPETIZERS

Spicy Lamb Meatballs
with Tahini Sauce

Sweet and Hot Glazed
Hazelnuts

Gorgonzola-Pear Tartlets

Brie Tartlets with Grape Salsa

Roasted Figs with Prosciutto

Chèvre and Sun-Dried
Tomato Tart

Crostini with Figs
and Goat Cheese

Crostini with Butternut Squash
and Prosciutto

Tuscan Bruschetta

Portobello and Gorgonzola
Crostini

Crabmeat Bruschetta

Beggar's Purse with Spiced
Ground Lamb

Beef Tenderloin
with Herbed Crostini

Pesto Chicken Spirals

Stuffed Mushroom Duxelles

Morel Mushroom Tempura

Dried Cherry and Chèvre
Wontons

Pulled Pork Lettuce Wraps

Three-Berry Meatball Martini

Bacon-Wrapped Dates
Stuffed with Goat Cheese

Spicy Lamb Meatballs with Tahini Sauce

Trium Winery | Talent, Oregon

Makes 12 meatballs

½ cup canned chickpeas, rinsed and drained

¾ pound ground lamb

¼ cup finely chopped shallots

½ cup finely chopped fresh cilantro

½ cup finely chopped fresh parsley

1 teaspoon kosher salt

1 teaspoon ground coriander

1 teaspoon ground cumin

½ teaspoon freshly ground black pepper

Pinch of ground cayenne pepper

½ cup canola oil for frying

Tahini Sauce (recipe follows)

In a medium bowl, mash the chickpeas with a fork. Mix in the lamb, shallots, cilantro, parsley, salt, coriander, cumin, black pepper, and cayenne pepper. Using your hands, form 1-inch meatballs.

Heat the canola oil in a large skillet over medium-high heat until it shimmers. Carefully cook the meatballs in batches (do not overcrowd the skillet), until crisp and golden brown and just cooked through, about 5 to 6 minutes. Transfer the meatballs to paper towels to drain.

Serve immediately with the Tahini Sauce.

Tahini Sauce

    1 cup tahini

    ½ cup canned chickpeas, rinsed and drained

    Juice of 1 lemon (about 3 tablespoons)

    2 tablespoons finely chopped shallots

    1 ¼ teaspoons kosher salt

    Pinch of ground cayenne pepper

In a food processor, mix the tahini, chickpeas, lemon juice, shallots, salt, and cayenne pepper. Slowly blend in ½ to ¾ cup water until the mixture is smooth. The sauce should be thinner than hummus but not runny. Adjust the seasonings to taste.

ADAPTED FROM A RECIPE IN *THE NEW YORK TIMES* BY MELISSA CLARK

. . . .

WINE PAIRING: *Trium Growers Cuvée*

A blend of Merlot, Cabernet Sauvignon, and Cabernet Franc, this wine provides layers of dark cherry and black currants, and a hint of earthiness. Flavors build and complement one another with subtle floral aromas.

Sweet and Hot Glazed Hazelnuts

Winter's Hill Vineyard | Lafayette, Oregon

Makes 2 cups

> 3 tablespoons Oregon honey
>
> 1 tablespoon butter, melted
>
> 1 ½ tablespoons sugar
>
> ½ teaspoon ground cinnamon
>
> ½ teaspoon ground cayenne pepper
>
> ½ teaspoon salt
>
> 2 cups shelled unsalted Oregon hazelnuts, skins removed

Preheat the oven to 300 degrees F.

In a medium bowl, mix together the honey, butter, sugar, cinnamon, cayenne pepper, and salt. Stir in the hazelnuts until evenly coated. Transfer the mixture to a baking sheet or a 9- by 13-inch baking pan. Spread the hazelnuts out evenly. Bake on the center rack in the oven for 30 to 45 minutes, jostling the baking sheet frequently, until all the hazelnuts are golden brown.

Remove the hazelnuts from the oven and place on a piece of aluminum foil. Let them cool for about 15 minutes, then break apart.

Serve right away or store in an airtight container for up to three days. If storing longer than that, reheat in the oven at 300 degrees F for 5 minutes to crisp.

COOK'S NOTE: To remove hazelnut skins, toast nuts in the oven at 375 degrees F for 10 minutes. Remove nuts, wrap them in a tea towel, and let them sit for 5 to 10 minutes. Vigorously rub the nuts against each other to remove most of their skins.

WINE PAIRING: *Winter's Hill White Gold Dessert Wine*

This strong and flavorful wine has intense flavors of honey, pears, and apples. An underlying spiciness leads to a crisp and refreshing finish. The nose has floral notes of white narcissus.

WINTER'S HILL VINEYARD

In the early 1960s, John and Lena Winter purchased a farm near Lafayette, Oregon. It became known as "Winter's Hill." Little did they know the area they moved to from Illinois would become ground zero for the Oregon wine industry, with such pioneers as Dick Erath and David Lett planting grapes within a decade.

The Winters' daughter, Emily, and her husband, Peter Gladhart, began planting a vineyard with their son, Russell, in 1990. They planted twelve acres of Pinot Noir and seven acres of Pinot Gris, Oregon's favorite red and white grapes. After a few years of selling their grapes to others, the Gladharts decided to produce their own wine, launching Winter's Hill Vineyard with the vaunted 1998 vintage.

Despite producing superior Pinot Noirs at modest prices, Winter's Hill has mostly flown under the radar, primarily because the Gladharts launched their winery the same time the Oregon wine industry hit a growth spurt. However, Winter's Hill has steadily gained a following, thanks to Pinot Noirs that show off the best of the Dundee Hills' "terroir": bright cherry and raspberry notes. Over the years Winter's Hill has expanded its offerings, adding a reserve-level Pinot Noir as well as Pinot Blanc, early Muscat, a Pinot Noir Rosé, and a late-harvest Pinot Gris.

Winter's Hill is well worth seeking out, especially for those who prefer more nicely priced wines. Winter's Hill's tasting room is near Lafayette, just a few minutes from the town of Dundee.

Gorgonzola-Pear Tartlets

Tytonidae Cellars | Walla Walla, Washington

Makes 30 tartlets

    3 ounces Gorgonzola cheese, softened

    3 ounces cream cheese, softened

    2 tablespoons light cream

    ⅛ teaspoon coarsely ground black or white pepper

    2 ripe pears (Anjou, Bartlett, or Bosc), peeled, cored, and diced

    Two 1.9-ounce packages frozen mini phyllo shells,
    thawed to room temperature

    ½ cup finely chopped pecans or walnuts

Preheat the oven to 350 degrees F.

In a medium bowl, mix together the Gorgonzola, cream cheese, light cream, and pepper until well combined. Stir in the pears. Arrange the phyllo shells on a baking sheet. Spoon in the pear mixture and sprinkle with the nuts.

Bake for 15 minutes, or until heated through. Serve warm.

....

WINE PAIRING: *Tytonidae Cellars Merlot Ice Wine*
This rich botrytised dessert wine with luxurious aromas and delicate flavors of honeyed apricot, mango, and lychee boasts a delicious and fresh balance of intense sweetness and refreshing acidity. Serve chilled for dessert or enjoy slow sipping as an apéritif.

Brie Tartlets with Grape Salsa

Chatter Creek Winery | Woodinville, Washington

Makes 30 appetizer servings

1 cup halved seedless red grapes

¼ teaspoon kosher salt

2 tablespoons finely chopped green onion (green part only)

1 tablespoon balsamic vinegar

2 teaspoons walnut oil or extra virgin olive oil

¼ teaspoon finely chopped fresh rosemary

¼ teaspoon minced garlic

⅛ teaspoon freshly ground black pepper

Two 1.9-ounce packages frozen mini phyllo shells, thawed to room temperature

⅔ cup finely chopped toasted walnuts

8 ounces Brie cheese, rind removed

Preheat the oven to 350 degrees F.

To make the grape salsa, pulse the grapes and salt in a food processor until the grapes are coarsely chopped (be careful not to overprocess). Transfer the grape mixture to a strainer and let strain for at least 10 minutes. In a small bowl, mix together the green onions, balsamic vinegar, walnut oil, rosemary, garlic, and pepper. Stir in the grape mixture and set aside.

Arrange the phyllo shells on a baking sheet. Fill each shell with a scant teaspoon of walnuts, a teaspoon of Brie, and a teaspoon of the grape salsa (use a fork to transfer the grape salsa to the phyllo shells to avoid capturing too much liquid). Bake the tartlets until the cheese begins to melt, about 5 minutes. Do not overbake. Serve immediately.

COOK'S NOTE: The grape salsa can be prepared up to one day in advance and refrigerated, but do not add the walnut oil mixture until ready to assemble. The tartlets can be partially assembled with the walnuts and the Brie up to 4 hours before serving. Top with the grape salsa and bake as directed.

....

WINE PAIRING: *Chatter Creek Viognier*
This wine presents clean flavors of apple and peach, with a hint of lychee fruit in its lingering finish. This wine is well balanced and a good match for lighter foods. It has a floral nose with hints of peach, pear, and melon.

Q: If an individual vineyard is listed on a label, what percentage of the grapes must have been grown at that vineyard?

A: At least 95 percent.

Roasted Figs with Prosciutto

Maryhill Winery | Goldendale, Washington

Makes 12 appetizer servings

> 12 fresh large ripe green figs (Adriatic or Kadota), stemmed
>
> 12 ½-inch cubes Dubliner Irish cheese (about 1 ½ ounces)
>
> 4 ounces prosciutto (about 12 slices)

Preheat the oven to 450 degrees F.

With a sharp knife, make a lengthwise slit into each fig, cutting three-quarters of the way through the fruit. Insert a cube of Dubliner Irish cheese into each fig and wrap with prosciutto.

Place the wrapped figs on a baking sheet. Roast in the center of the oven until the prosciutto is crisp on the edges and the fig is warmed through, about 12 minutes.

....

WINE PAIRING: *Maryhill Classic Sangiovese*
Lively and spicy, this Italian varietal has aromas of black cherry, cinnamon, and rose hips. The palate is smooth and filled with ripe plum and pomegranate, finishing with fresh pepper and cherry.

MARYHILL WINERY

In every sense, Maryhill Winery may be perfectly perched for success. The winery near Goldendale, Washington, in the eastern Columbia Gorge, launched with the 1999 vintage and has not slowed down since. Just west of the famed and eclectic Maryhill Museum, Maryhill Winery sits atop a cliff overlooking the dramatic Gorge, with the mighty Columbia River flowing below and majestic Mount Hood rising to the southwest. Sipping wine and taking in a concert or enjoying a picnic could not be much more perfect than at Maryhill.

Owners Craig and Vicki Leuthold were successful in Spokane business and equally as successful at transferring their skills to Maryhill. First, they found the perfect spot for their winery, then hired great winemakers, and finally used their marketing prowess to bring in the fans. Along the way, they built a four-thousand-seat amphitheater that attracts crowds from throughout the Pacific Northwest for top musical acts.

In 2002, Maryhill entered its Zinfandel—a rare wine for Washington at the time—in the West Coast Wine Competition. Not only did it win a gold medal, but it also earned best Zinfandel of the judging, and this was in the heart of California Zinfandel country. This victory spurred the Leutholds to expand their Zinfandel production, and it encouraged other wineries to look at the California-centric grape, often with great success. In a short period of time, Maryhill has gone from an idea to one of Washington's most successful and visible family-owned wineries, acquiring honors such as "Washington Winery of the Year" (*Wine Press Northwest*) and "Best Destination Winery" (*Seattle magazine*).

Chèvre and Sun-Dried Tomato Tart

Chinook Wines | Prosser, Washington

Makes 36 appetizer servings

- 1 teaspoon plus 2 tablespoons olive oil, divided
- ⅔ cup coarsely ground yellow cornmeal
- ⅓ cup all purpose flour
- 1 tablespoon sugar
- ¼ teaspoon salt
- ¼ teaspoon baking powder
- ½ cup buttermilk
- 2 eggs, divided
- 1 clove garlic, minced
- 5 to 6 sun-dried tomatoes in oil, drained and diced
- 4 ounces soft goat cheese (chèvre)
- 2 ounces light cream cheese, softened
- 3 baby zucchini, cut into thin slices
- 1 tablespoon Parmesan cheese
- 2 teaspoons finely chopped fresh basil or thyme leaves

Preheat the oven to 375 degrees F.

Grease a 7- by 11-inch or 9-inch-square glass baking dish with 1 teaspoon of the olive oil.

In a medium bowl, mix the cornmeal, flour, sugar, salt, and baking powder. In another bowl, whisk together the remaining 2 tablespoons of the olive oil, the buttermilk, one of the eggs, and the garlic. Add this to the cornmeal-flour mixture. Stir in the sun-dried tomatoes and be careful not to overbeat.

Pour the batter into the greased baking dish and bake on the center rack in the oven for 8 to 10 minutes, or until golden brown.

Meanwhile, in a small bowl, beat the goat cheese, light cream cheese, and the remaining egg until smooth. Spread the goat cheese mixture evenly over the cooked warm crust. Top with zucchini slices, Parmesan, and basil. Return to the oven for 10 minutes, or until the zucchini is tender.

Cut into bite-size squares and serve warm.

....

WINE PAIRING: *Chinook Yakima Valley Sauvignon Blanc*
Blended with 10 percent Sémillon to add depth and flavor, this wine is balanced with a crisp finish. Pair with herb, vegetables, citrus, and seafood dishes.

CHINOOK WINES

With all the hype for the Walla Walla Valley, Red Mountain, and Woodinville, the Yakima Valley often seems to be left out of the conversation. In the heart of this valley where the Washington wine industry was born is one of finest producers. Kay Simon and Clay Mackey are the husband-wife team behind Chinook, a best-kept secret for Washington wine lovers. The couple launched Chinook in 1983 after working for Chateau Ste. Michelle for many years. Simon hired Doug Gore, who became Columbia Crest's winemaker and now oversees operations for all of Ste. Michelle Wine Estates.

Mackey's expertise is on the viticulture side, where he manages the estate and purchases grapes.

Simon focuses on balance. Rarely are her wines high in alcohol, even coming from the hot Red Mountain appellation. Her Cabernet Sauvignons, Cabernet Francs, and Merlots define elegance. Her Sauvignon Blancs and Sémillons are classic, and her dry Rosé, made from Cabernet Franc has a near-cult following. The pair are accomplished cooks with a passion for local ingredients. An invitation to dine at Chinook should not be turned down, as the experience is guaranteed to inspire the mind and the taste buds.

That might be one of the secrets to their wines: If you love cooking as much as Simon and Mackey do, you want wines that will pair perfectly.

Crostini with Figs and Goat Cheese

Benson Vineyards Estate Winery | Manson, Washington

Makes 20 appetizer servings

> 2 cups Benson Vineyards Estate Syrah or other dry red wine
>
> 20 dried figs (about ½ pound), stemmed and halved (or quartered if large)
>
> 1 artisan baguette, cut on the diagonal into 20 slices (about ½-inch thick)
>
> 8 ounces herbed goat cheese (chèvre)
>
> 4 ounces prosciutto (about 10 slices, cut in half)

Preheat the oven to 350 degrees F.

In a small saucepan, bring the wine and the figs to a simmer over medium-low heat. Simmer uncovered for about 20 minutes, or until the figs have absorbed most of the wine and they are tender and plump. Remove the figs with a slotted spoon to a bowl, and reserve for later. Increase the heat to medium-high and continue to simmer the wine until it is reduced to a syrupy liquid. Set aside.

Arrange the baguette slices on a baking sheet. Toast lightly in the oven, about 4 minutes on each side.

Remove the baguette slices from the oven. Spread the herbed goat cheese on the slices, then top with a quarter to a half slice of the prosciutto, rolled to fit on top of the cheese. Place the fig halves on top of the rolled-up prosciutto.

Serve at room temperature or heat in the oven for 5 minutes until warm. Drizzle with a small amount of the reserved wine reduction.

....

WINE PAIRING: *Benson Vineyards Estate Syrah*
This Syrah is full-bodied with hearty berry, black currant, smoky black pepper, and fig flavors. Dark, rich, and well-balanced, it has an elegant finish.

Crostini with Butternut Squash and Prosciutto

Flying Trout Wines | Walla Walla, Washington

Makes 18 appetizer servings

> 1 butternut squash, halved and seeded
>
> 4 tablespoons butter, melted, divided
>
> ¼ cup light cream
>
> 1 teaspoon ground cumin
>
> 1 artisan baguette, cut on the diagonal into 18 slices (about ½-inch thick)
>
> 1 tablespoon minced garlic
>
> Salt
>
> 3 ounces prosciutto (about 9 slices)
>
> 9 fresh sage leaves (cut into thin strips if desired)

Preheat the oven to 425 degrees F.

Brush each squash half with ½ tablespoon of melted butter, then wrap in aluminum foil. Bake in a glass dish for 1 hour, or until the squash is soft and tender. Remove the squash from the oven, unwrap, and let cool slightly. Scoop the squash from the skin. In a medium bowl, mash the squash with the light cream and cumin. Cover and keep warm.

Arrange the baguette slices on a baking sheet and brush with the remaining melted butter. Top each with a little minced garlic and salt. Bake 6 to 7 minutes, or until golden brown.

Place the prosciutto slices on the crostini. Top with a spoonful of the warm squash purée and the sage leaves.

WINE PAIRING: *Flying Trout Non-Vintage Deep River Red*
This beefy, rustic red has flavors of cocoa, coffee, and black cherry, with notes of cloves, blueberry, and thyme. Velvety, with strong tannins and a lingering finish, this wine is best enjoyed with food.

Q: To what does "Estate Bottled" refer?

A: It means that 100 percent of the grapes have been grown on land owned or controlled by the winery in the viticultural area.

Tuscan Bruschetta

Covington Cellars | Woodinville, Washington

Makes 24 appetizer servings

- 2 large or 3 medium leeks (white and light green parts only), washed and patted dry
- 2 tablespoons butter
- 5 ounces prosciutto, cut into ¼- by ½-inch strips
- 2 cloves garlic, minced
- 1 artisan baguette, cut on the diagonal into 24 slices (about ½ -inch thick)
- 4 ounces soft goat cheese (chèvre)

Preheat the oven to 400 degrees F.

Cut the leeks in half lengthwise and remove the outer layer. Cut horizontally to make half circles, about ⅛-inch thick. Put the leeks in a bowl of water to clean and strain in a colander.

Heat the butter in a medium skillet over medium heat. Add the leeks, cook and stir until wilted, about 5 minutes. Add the prosciutto, cook and stir 8 to 10 minutes. Add the garlic, stirring another 2 to 3 minutes until the leeks are tender. Remove from heat and keep warm.

Just before serving, arrange the baguette slices on a baking sheet. Lightly toast on the center rack in the oven, approximately 3 minutes on each side. Spread the goat cheese on the baguette slices while hot and top with the warm leek mixture. Serve immediately.

....

WINE PAIRING: *Covington Cellars Tuscan Red*
A Super Tuscan-blend of Sangiovese, Cabernet Sauvignon, and Cabernet Franc, this wine has vibrant fruit notes, great structure, and elegant balance.

Portobello and Gorgonzola Crostini

Lost River Winery | Mazama, Washington

Makes 18 appetizer servings

       3 tablespoons butter

       2 cloves garlic, minced

       8 ounces fresh Portobello mushrooms, stemmed and diced

       ½ cup heavy cream

       ½ cup (2 ounces) crumbled Gorgonzola cheese

       3 ounces prosciutto (about 9 slices), cut into ¼- by ½-inch strips

       Sea salt and freshly ground black pepper

       1 artisan baguette, cut on the diagonal into 18 slices (about ½-inch thick)

       Fresh Italian parsley, minced

Preheat the oven to 375 degrees F.

Melt the butter in a large saucepan over medium-high heat. Add the garlic and mushrooms; cook and stir for about 10 minutes, or until the mushrooms are cooked through and brown. Add the heavy cream and bring to a boil. Boil until the liquid is completely absorbed, about 4 minutes. Remove from heat. Stir in the Gorgonzola and mix until the cheese melts. Add the prosciutto, stirring until combined. Season to taste with sea salt and pepper. Arrange the baguette slices on a baking sheet. Bake on the center rack in the oven until golden brown, about 5 minutes. Top each crostini with 1 tablespoon of the mushroom mixture. Bake crostini until heated through, about 6 minutes. Sprinkle with the parsley and serve immediately.

COOK'S NOTE: The mushroom topping can be made one day ahead. Cover and refrigerate, then top crostini before baking.

RECIPE CONTRIBUTED BY DEB THORLAKSON

WINE PAIRING: *Lost River Columbia Valley Rainshadow*

A white Bordeaux-style blend of Sauvignon Blanc and Sémillon, this wine exhibits aromas of citrus, pear, and tropical fruits with crisp acidity.

LOST RIVER WINERY

John Morgan and Barbara House relocated from Whatcom County to Washington's breathtaking Methow Valley, a region of the state that still is relatively undiscovered by the masses—and very far away from vineyards. The two moved to the tiny town of Mazama in 2001, after spending seven years working on a house there. Morgan had grown up in a home that appreciated the great wines of Bordeaux, Burgundy, and Napa, so he was bit by the winemaking bug at an early age. In early 2002, the couple began working on their winery and had everything in place for that fall's harvest. As they continue to do today, Morgan and House received those first grapes from growers in the Columbia,

Yakima, and Walla Walla valleys, Horse Heaven Hills, and Wahluke Slope.

That first vintage was a huge hit, as the Lost River 2002 Merlot won best in show at the 2004 Tri-Cities Wine Festival, a competition that included more than two hundred wineries from throughout the Pacific Northwest. They followed that up with a gold medal in the prestigious Los Angeles International Wine Competition for the 2003 Syrah. Since then, the accolades have continued to roll in. Today, Lost River Winery has expanded its offerings to more than a half-dozen wines, focusing primarily on reds. With its early track record, expect Lost River to remain a winery to keep an eye on.

Crabmeat Bruschetta

Natalie's Estate Winery | Newberg, Oregon

Makes 16 appetizer servings

    1 artisan baguette, cut on the diagonal into 16 slices (about ½-inch thick)

    ⅓ cup extra virgin olive oil

    3 tablespoons mayonnaise

    1 tablespoon Dijon mustard

    1 tablespoon fresh lime juice

    1 tablespoon chopped fresh Italian parsley

    1 tablespoon chopped fresh chives

    1 teaspoon grated Parmesan cheese

    ½ teaspoon ground cayenne pepper

    ½ teaspoon ground paprika

    Drop of hot pepper sauce

    1 cup (6½ ounces) cooked Dungeness crabmeat

    ½ cup diced red bell pepper

    Fresh Italian parsley or chives, chopped

Preheat the broiler.

Lightly brush both sides of the baguette slices with the olive oil. Arrange them on a baking sheet and broil until golden brown, about 2 minutes per side.

Preheat the oven to 425 degrees F.

In a medium bowl, mix together the mayonnaise, mustard, lime juice, parsley, chives, Parmesan, cayenne pepper, paprika, and pepper sauce. Gently stir in the crabmeat and red bell pepper. Spread approximately 1 tablespoon of the crab mixture onto each baguette slice. Bake for 5 minutes. Sprinkle with parsley and serve immediately.

WINE PAIRING: *Natalie's Estate Elephant Mountain Viognier*
Citrus, melon, and floral aromas lead to a rich concentration of honeysuckle and apricot flavors with a touch of crispness on the finish. This pairs well with any shellfish dish.

Q: What is cooking wine?

A: Cooking wine is usually a very ordinary wine to which salt has been added. Chefs generally recommend that you avoid cooking wine when cooking; rather, cook with a wine that you enjoy drinking.

Beggar's Purse with Spiced Ground Lamb

àMaurice Cellars | Walla Walla, Washington

Makes 24 appetizer servings

> 1¾ pounds ground lamb
>
> 1 cup finely chopped Walla Walla sweet onion
>
> 1 teaspoon minced garlic
>
> ⅛ teaspoon ground cinnamon
>
> ⅛ teaspoon finely crushed fennel seed
>
> ½ teaspoon salt
>
> 4 ounces light cream cheese, softened
>
> Non-stick olive oil cooking spray
>
> One 16-ounce box frozen phyllo dough (about 20 sheets), thawed to room temperature

Preheat the oven to 350 degrees F.

In a large saucepan, cook the lamb, onion, and garlic over medium heat, stirring frequently and breaking up large pieces of meat, until the lamb is brown. Mix in the cinnamon, fennel seed, and salt. Remove from heat and let cool for 10 minutes. Stir in the light cream cheese and set aside.

Spray a baking sheet with cooking spray.

Unroll the phyllo dough on a clean kitchen cloth and cover with wax paper or a lightly dampened cloth to prevent the dough from drying out. Place one sheet of phyllo dough on a smooth dry surface and spray with olive oil cooking spray. Place a second sheet on top of first and spray with olive oil cooking spray. Repeat with three more layers, spraying the top sheet well. Cut the phyllo stack into 4-inch squares.

Place a heaping tablespoon of lamb mixture in the center of each square. Take one corner and the opposite corner and pinch them together just above the filling, letting the tops stay loose and ruffle a bit. Then pinch together the other two opposite corners in the same way. Repeat with the remaining sheets of phyllo.

Put the phyllo bundles on the prepared baking sheet, and spray them lightly with cooking spray. Place the baking sheet on the oven rack just below the center. Bake for 7 to 10 minutes, or until golden brown. Serve hot.

COOK'S NOTE: While assembling each Beggar's Purse, don't try to be perfect—once baked, they have a unique charm all of their own. They can be assembled ahead of time and stored in the freezer for up to three weeks. Remove from freezer about 1½ hours before baking.

....

WINE PAIRING: *àMaurice Cellars Malbec, Columbia Valley*
This wine has fabulous full tannins with flavors of plum and other dark fruits, along with some mineral character. A little toast from the barrel nestles between African passion fruit and huckleberries to please and tease the palate.

Beef Tenderloin with Herbed Crostini

Fielding Hills Winery | East Wenatchee, Washington

Makes 20 appetizer servings

    ⅓ cup extra virgin olive oil

    ½ teaspoon dried marjoram

    ½ teaspoon dried thyme leaves

    ½ teaspoon dried rosemary

    ½ teaspoon dried oregano

    ¼ teaspoon dried basil

    ¼ teaspoon dried sage

    1 artisan baguette, cut on the diagonal into 20 slices (about ½-inch thick)

    1 beef tenderloin (about ¾ pound), trimmed and patted dry

    1 pound (4 sticks) butter

    Sea salt

Preheat the oven to 350 degrees F.

In a small bowl, mix together the olive oil, marjoram, thyme, rosemary, oregano, basil, and sage. Set aside.

Arrange the baguette slices on a baking sheet covered with aluminum foil. Brush them with the olive oil–herb mixture and bake for 8 to 10 minutes, or until toasted. Remove from the oven and set aside.

Increase the oven temperature to 500 degrees F.

Sear the tenderloin in a very hot skillet until all sides have been browned. Place the meat on a baking sheet covered with foil and bake on the center rack in the oven for approximately 15 minutes, or until the meat reaches an internal temperature of between 135 and 140 degrees F. Remove the roast, tent with foil, and let stand for 15 minutes. The internal temperature will rise 5 degrees to 140 degrees F (rare) or to 145 degrees F (medium rare).

Melt the butter in a medium saucepan and keep warm. Cut the tenderloin into bite-size medallions and dip in the melted butter. Place one tenderloin medallion on each herbed crostini. Sprinkle with sea salt and serve immediately.

RECIPE CONTRIBUTED BY MISSION STREET BISTRO

WINE PAIRING: *Fielding Hills Syrah*

This Syrah is supple and heady with dark berry, violet, bacon, and cinnamon aromas and flavors with hints of pepper and clove. It has underlying buttery notes with well-integrated tannins and a long finish.

FIELDING HILLS WINERY

After earning a BA in business, Mike Wade went home to run a family-owned cherry- and apple-packing warehouse and orchard started by his grandfather, Isham Fielding Wade. Mike preferred beer to wine, but at a dinner in the 1980s, Mike had a life-changing experience; a glass of house burgundy paired with prime rib became a revelation into the world of wine appreciation. His interest skyrocketed in the 1990s during a Napa Valley tour. When Wade returned home, he and his wife, Karen, traveled around Eastern Washington, looking at vineyard operations—always with an eye toward turning their passion into a business.

In a move to diversify crops, Mike added vineyards to the family business in 1998. Red Delicious Apples were pulled out to make way for Merlot, Syrah, Cabernet Franc, and Cabernet Sauvignon grapes on family-owned land in the Wahluke Slope. The first crush from Riverbend Vineyard was in the fall of 2000 and named after his grandfather. Fielding Hills Winery was born.

The initial wines—a Cabernet Sauvignon, a Merlot, and a red blend—were stunning when they released in 2002. Fielding Hills Winery is now recognized as one of the rising stars in the State of Washington. After the first vintage was released, Mike added Syrah and Cabernet Franc to the lineup.

Located in the Wenatchee Valley, Fielding Hills Winery was one of the first to open in this region. The Wades and Fielding Hills have led the way, as the area has exploded with dozens of wineries today.

Pesto Chicken Spirals

Rosella's Vineyard and Winery | Grants Pass, Oregon

Makes 30 spirals

    1 pound ground chicken

    ¼ cup chopped ham

    One 16-ounce frozen puff pastry, thawed to room temperature and halved

    ¼ cup prepared basil pesto (store-bought or homemade)

    ½ cup grated Asiago or Parmesan cheese

    Creamy Pesto Sauce (recipe follows)

In a large skillet, cook the chicken over medium heat until it is no longer pink inside. Finely mince the ham or place in a food processor and pulse until it is ground fine (but not mushy). Add the ham to the chicken and mix thoroughly.

On a floured surface, roll the pastry into two 10- by 14-inch rectangles. Spread each rectangle with 2 tablespoons of the pesto, leaving a 1-inch border around the edges. Spread the meat mixture evenly over the pesto. Sprinkle with the Asiago.

Starting at the short end, roll each rectangle into a tight pinwheel. Wrap each roll in parchment paper and put in the freezer for 30 minutes to firm it up.

Preheat the oven to 425 degrees F.

Remove the rolls from the freezer and cut into ½-inch-thick slices. Place the slices on a parchment lined baking sheet. Bake on the center rack in the oven for 15 to 16 minutes, or until golden and crisp.

Arrange the spirals on a serving platter. Drizzle with the Creamy Pesto Sauce.

COOK'S NOTE: The spirals can be made ahead of time. Place uncooked spirals in a resealable freezer bag and store in freezer for up to three weeks. Thaw spirals before baking.

Creamy Pesto Sauce

      3 tablespoons butter

      2 tablespoons prepared pesto (store-bought or homemade)

      6 tablespoons heavy cream

      2 tablespoons grated Parmesan cheese

In a small saucepan, melt the butter over medium heat. Stir in the pesto, heavy cream, and Parmesan. Lower the temperature and simmer uncovered until reduced to a desirable drizzling consistency.

WINE PAIRING: *Rosella's Unoaked Chardonnay*

Unoaked, to express full-fruit flavor, this wine is clean and crisp. It possesses a very citrus quality, specifically that of grapefruit, and is well-balanced, making it very food friendly.

Q: What's the quickest way to chill a bottle of wine?

A: An ice bucket filled with water and ice will chill a bottle of wine in less than 15 minutes; chilling wine in the refrigerator will take closer to an hour.

Stuffed Mushroom Duxelles

Reininger Winery | Walla Walla, Washington

Makes 30 appetizer servings

> 1½ pounds (about 40 medium) fresh cremini mushrooms, divided
>
> 4 large sprigs fresh thyme, divided
>
> 2 tablespoons butter
>
> 1 tablespoon Extra-virgin olive oil
>
> 1 small shallot, minced
>
> 1 clove garlic, minced
>
> ¼ cup heavy cream
>
> Salt and freshly ground black pepper
>
> 8 ounces mascarpone cheese (or cream cheese)
>
> 2 tablespoons grated Parmigiano-Reggiano cheese

Preheat the oven to 350 degrees F.

Finely mince ten of the mushrooms (stems and caps) or pulse in a food processor until finely chopped. (Do not turn into pulp, as the mushrooms need some texture.) Remove stems from the remaining mushrooms and set aside. Mince the leaves of two of the sprigs of thyme and set aside.

Heat the butter and olive oil in a saucepan over medium heat. Add the shallot; cook and stir until opaque, about 3 minutes.

Turn the heat down to low and add the minced mushrooms and a pinch of salt. Stir the mixture frequently for 10 minutes. Add the garlic and the minced thyme and continue cooking until the mushrooms are fragrant and have given up most of their moisture, about 8 to 10 minutes.

Increase the heat to medium and slowly stir the heavy cream into the mushroom mixture, 1 tablespoon at a time. Cook until the heavy cream is reduced and the duxelles is firm and moist but not wet (pinch a little between your fingers to gauge), about 8 minutes. Season with salt and pepper to taste. If making ahead, let the mixture cool slightly, then refrigerate.

On a baking sheet, toss the reserved mushroom caps with a drizzle of olive oil, a sprinkle of salt and pepper, and the remaining two sprigs of thyme. Bake on the center rack in the oven for 10 to 12 minutes, stirring every 5 minutes, until they are tender and cooked through. If making ahead, let the mushroom caps cool slightly, then refrigerate.

Preheat the oven to 500 degrees F.

Fill each mushroom cap with the duxelles, just until it is even with the top of the mushroom. Arrange them on a baking sheet and top each mushroom cap with mascarpone (a dollop about two-thirds the size of the mushroom top). Sprinkle with the Parmigiano-Reggiano cheese.

Bake on the center rack in the oven for 3 to 5 minutes, or until the mushrooms turn slightly golden brown. Transfer to a serving platter and garnish with thyme sprigs.

RECIPE CONTRIBUTED BY JOHN LASTOSKIE

....

WINE PAIRING: *Reininger Merlot, Walla Walla Valley*
An elegant, velvety Merlot with concentrated flavors of chocolate, espresso, and spice. This wine has lush black currant and supple plum notes and a polished finish of dried cherries dipped in chocolate.

REININGER WINERY

Chuck Reininger is used to reaching new heights. Before becoming one of the Walla Walla Valley's most respected winemakers, Reininger was a mountain-climbing guide who spent nearly as much time on Mount Rainier as off it. He and his wife, Tracy Tucker, moved to her hometown of Walla Walla, and Chuck took a harvest job at Waterbrook Winery in nearby Lowden. After that, he was hooked.

With Tracy, he launched Reininger Winery in 1997 and now crafts highly sought-after red wines, particularly Cabernet Sauvignon, Syrah, and Merlot—all using grapes from the Walla Walla Valley.

In 2003, Chuck and Tracy partnered with Tracy's brothers, Kelly and Jay, and began renovating two large potato sheds into a spacious new facility just west of Walla Walla, along Highway 12.

Shortly after moving, the family announced Helix, a new label of wines using grapes from the broad Columbia Valley. The wines are named for the Eastern Oregon town of Helix, where Tracy's family raised wheat for three generations. That farm, when sold, financed the new winery and launch of the new label.

Now in its second decade, Reininger Winery stands out in an ever-more-crowded Walla Walla wine scene as one of the state's finest producers. Its wines exude elegance over boldness, sophistication over power. Thus they taste wonderful upon release and also age perfectly for years—a rare combination. All of this, from a guy who used to climb mountains for a living.

Morel Mushroom Tempura

Zefina Winery | Seattle, Washington

Makes 4 appetizer servings

15 ounces fresh morel mushrooms

2 eggs, beaten

¾ cup whole milk

1 tablespoon minced fresh Italian parsley

1 teaspoon fine sea salt

1 teaspoon freshly ground black and white pepper blend

1 cup panko (Japanese bread crumbs) or coarse dry bread crumbs

½ cup peanut oil or grapeseed oil for frying

Clean the mushrooms by immersing them in salt water, then drain using a colander and gently pat dry with paper towels.

In a small bowl, whisk the eggs, milk, parsley, salt, and pepper. Put the panko in another bowl. Dip the mushrooms in the egg mixture, then toss in the panko.

Heat the peanut oil in a large skillet to 350 degrees F. You will know the oil is hot enough when you place a drop of water in it and it sizzles loudly. Carefully place the coated mushrooms in the skillet. Cook the mushrooms until they are golden brown on the bottom, then flip them over to brown the other side. When the mushrooms are evenly browned, remove them from the pan using a slotted spoon and drain them on a paper towel.

Arrange the tempura on a platter and serve with cocktail toothpicks.

RECIPE CONTRIBUTED BY JEANIE INGLIS-CHOWANIETZ

Delicious dark fruit and a background of spice give this wine a pleasing palate with a backbone of fine tannins and lively acidity. There are aromas of buttered popcorn, dark dried cherries, dried figs, and a hint of dried basil.

Q: How many ounces are in one bottle of wine, and how many glasses is this equivalent to?

A: A bottle of wine contains 25.6 ounces which will yield about five 5-ounce glasses.

Dried Cherry and Chèvre Wontons

Gamache Vintners | Prosser, Washington

Makes 24 appetizer servings

    1 cup dried cherries

    ¼ cup dried cranberries

    ¼ cup beef stock

    ¼ cup Gamache Vintners Cabernet Sauvignon or other dry red wine

    3 slices bacon, cut into small pieces

    2 cloves garlic, finely diced

    2 shallots, finely diced

    4 ounces soft goat cheese (chèvre)

    One 14-ounce package wonton wrappers

    3 cups peanut oil or safflower oil for frying

In a medium saucepan, bring the cherries, cranberries, beef stock, and wine to a simmer, then remove from heat. Let the mixture stand uncovered for 15 minutes, allowing the dried fruit to rehydrate.

Meanwhile, in a small skillet, cook the bacon over medium-high heat until golden and crispy. Add the garlic and shallots, stirring frequently until fragrant, about 2 minutes. Combine the bacon mixture and the fruit mixture in a food processor until coarsely blended.

To assemble the wontons, place a scant teaspoon of the fruit mixture and a scant teaspoon of the chèvre in the center of a wonton wrapper. Fold the wonton into a triangle. Moisten one end using your finger dipped in water and pinch the two ends firmly together.

Heat the peanut oil in a wok or 10-inch skillet over high heat until a haze forms above the oil or it registers 375 degrees F on a deep-frying thermometer. Deep-fry the wontons, six or eight at a time, for 2 minutes, or until they are crisp and golden brown. Transfer to paper towels to drain. Repeat for the remaining wontons. Serve warm.

....

WINE PAIRING: *Gamache Vintners Cabernet Sauvignon*
This is a cellar-worthy wine loaded with ripe cherry, fresh plum, and black olive flavors. Sweet tannins and balanced acidity give this wine food-worthy structure.

GAMACHE VINTNERS

Brothers Bob and Roger Gamache planted their first wine grapes in the early 1980s in the little farming community of Basin City, Washington, a town like so many others that would not be much more than sagebrush and grassland were it not for the Columbia Basin Project that brought irrigation to Eastern Washington's shrub steppe region. For many years the brothers concentrated on growing such fine grapes as Cabernet Sauvignon, Merlot, and Syrah for winemakers.

Not content with staying only in viticulture, the brothers hatched a plan to create a winery and Gamache Vintners was born with the 2002 vintage, some two decades after the fourth-generation farmers put their first vines in the soil. They hired Charlie Hoppes, a winemaker whose resume included Ste. Michelle, Three Rivers, and his own

Fidelitas, and the first wines were produced at Cañon de Sol, a small winery near Richland, where Charlie also made the wines. As one might expect with such pedigree, the wines have been an instant hit, winning medals at professional judgings and earning accolades from critics and the public alike.

Their Prosser-based tasting room opened in August 2009 in Vintners Village. The brothers offer an ever-widening array of wines, from Cabernet Sauvignon to Merlot to Syrah to blends. They've released a Viognier and Riesling on the white side and even produced a Cabernet that blends their estate fruit with that of their cousin, famed grape grower Paul Champoux of Champoux Vineyards. Gamache is one of Washington's rising wine stars.

Pulled Pork Lettuce Wraps

North Shore Wine Cellars | Bingen, Washington

Makes 18 wraps

>   2 pork shoulder steaks (about 1¾ pounds)
>
>   ½ cup plus 1 tablespoon extra virgin olive oil, divided
>
>   2 cloves garlic, minced, divided
>
>   3 tablespoons brown sugar
>
>   1 tablespoon ground ginger
>
>   Salt and freshly ground black pepper
>
>   ½ yellow onion, chopped
>
>   1 teaspoon chopped fresh rosemary
>
>   2 cups North Shore Wine Cellars Barrel Aged Cherry Wine or other fruity red wine
>
>   1 tablespoon granulated sugar
>
>   18 hearts of romaine lettuce leaves, washed and patted dry
>
>   1 cup crumbled feta cheese

Place the pork in a shallow glass or ceramic baking dish and cover with a ½ cup of the olive oil, half of the garlic, the brown sugar, ginger, and salt and pepper to taste Cover and refrigerate for 4 hours or overnight.

Remove the pork from the refrigerator 45 minutes before preparing.

Preheat the oven to 325 degrees F.

Add ¼ cup water to the baking dish and cover tightly with aluminum foil. Bake in the middle of the oven until very tender, 1¾ to 2 hours. Allow the pork to cool, then shred the meat with a fork or using your fingers. Discard the bones and excess fat.

While the shredded pork cools, heat the remaining olive oil over medium heat in a medium saucepan. Add the onion and the remaining garlic, and cook until softened, about 5 minutes. Add the rosemary and stir for 1 minute. Pour in the wine and sugar and bring to boil. Simmer uncovered until the liquid is reduced by half, about 20 minutes. Season to taste with salt and pepper; set aside.

Arrange the romaine leaves on a serving platter. Top each with shredded pork, crumbled feta, and a drizzle of the wine reduction.

....

WINE PAIRING: *North Shore Wine Cellars Barrel Aged Cherry Wine*
A semisweet table wine with pleasing notes of Bing cherry. Rich and full-bodied with floral aromas, this wine tastes best chilled or at room temperature.

Three-Berry Meatball Martini

Troon Vineyard | Grants Pass, Oregon

Makes 8 appetizer servings

    ½ pound ground Italian sausage

    ½ pound ground beef

    1 small yellow onion, minced

    1 teaspoon freshly ground black pepper

    1 teaspoon seasoned salt

    1 teaspoon minced garlic

    1 tablespoon vegetable oil

    Three-Berry Sauce (recipe follows)

In a medium bowl, mix together the Italian sausage, ground beef, onion, pepper, seasoned salt, and minced garlic. Using your hands, roll the meat mixture into golf ball-size balls. Put them on a waxed paper–lined baking sheet. Cover with waxed paper and refrigerate for 30 minutes.

Preheat the oven to 350 degrees F.

Heat the oil in a large nonstick skillet. Pan-fry the meatballs until they are browned on all sides. Spray a baking sheet with nonstick cooking spray. Transfer the meatballs with the pan juices into the prepared pan. Bake on the center rack in the oven for 30 minutes, stirring halfway through, until the centers are no longer pink and the internal temperature reaches 165 degrees F.

To serve, ladle a small amount of the Three-Berry Sauce in the bottom of a martini glass, thread three meatballs on a 6-inch bamboo skewer, and place the skewer in the martini glass.

Three-Berry Sauce

1 cup heavy cream

1 cup assorted fresh or frozen berries (blueberries, raspberries, blackberries, lingonberries, or marionberries)

1 cup berry preserves (any kind)

Heat the heavy cream, berries, and preserves in a medium saucepan over medium heat, until the preserves are melted and the mixture is hot. If desired, run an immersion blender through the mixture to produce a smoother sauce. Keep warm.

COOK'S NOTE: Frozen berries will impart more intense flavors in the sauce, but fresh berries provide more silkiness.

....

WINE PAIRING: *Troon Vineyard Druid's Fluid*

This slightly sweet, fruity red blend is ultra-smooth and easy to drink. Full of ripe fruit such as fresh Bing cherry, blackberry, currant, and plum, it's a perfect wine to drink young.

Bacon-Wrapped Dates Stuffed with Goat Cheese

Gifford Hirlinger | Walla Walla, Washington

Makes 24 appetizer servings

    24 dried whole Medjool dates

    6 ounces soft goat cheese (chèvre)

    1 pound thick-cut bacon (about 12 slices), halved

Preheat the oven to 400 degrees F.

Slice each date lengthwise and remove the pit. Stuff the date cavity with goat cheese, put the dates back together, and wrap the dates with bacon. Arrange the dates on a baking sheet. Bake on the center rack for 20 minutes, or until the bacon is fully cooked. Serve warm.

....

WINE PAIRING: *Gifford Hirlinger Stateline Red*
This graceful blend of Merlot and Cabernet Sauvignon fills the mouth with bright cherry and raspberries. It is a delicate, versatile, food-friendly wine.

OFF THE GRILL

Blue Cheese Cabernet
Tri-Tips with Mushrooms

Tenderloin Bruschetta with
Horseradish and Blue Cheese

Prawns and Mango Salsa Cocktail

Portobello Mushrooms
with Green Peppercorn Sauce

Grilled Asparagus with Walla
Walla Sweet Spring Onions

Masa with White Beans,
Pancetta, and Arugula

Prosciutto-Wrapped Grilled
Shrimp

Raspberry Glazed Pork Bites

Spot Prawn Kabobs
with Black Currant Chutney

Grilled Coconut Curry Ceviche

Blackberry Chipotle
Sockeye Salmon

Grilled Salmon with Hazelnut–
Brown Butter Sauce

Lamb Skewers with Yogurt
Cucumber Dipping Sauce

Herbed Lamb Chops
with Syrah Reduction

Smoky Flat Iron Steak Bites
with Chimichurri Sauce

Grilled Oysters with
Cranberry Salsa

Grilled Asparagus
Chèvre Tartines

Blue Cheese Cabernet Tri-Tips with Mushrooms

Challenger Ridge Winery | Concrete, Washington

Makes 6 small plate servings

2 tablespoons extra virgin olive oil

4 cloves garlic, crushed

4 cups Challenger Ridge Cabernet Sauvignon or other dry red wine

½ cup (1 stick) butter, softened

2 tablespoons crumbled blue cheese

4 tri-tip steaks (about 6 ounces each and 1-inch thick), excess fat trimmed

1 cup sliced white mushrooms

Preheat the grill to medium heat.

Heat the olive oil in a large skillet over low heat. Add the garlic; cook and stir until the garlic is infused into oil, about 2 minutes. Pour in the wine and simmer uncovered until reduced to 1½ cups, about 25 to 30 minutes. Set aside.

In a small bowl, mash together the butter and blue cheese. Set aside. Grill the steaks 6 to 8 minutes per side for medium-rare. Transfer the meat to a cutting board and spread the butter–blue cheese mixture over the steaks. Cover them with aluminum foil for 10 minutes to let rest.

Just before serving, add the mushrooms to the wine reduction. Stir over medium heat for about 5 minutes, or until mushrooms are heated through.

To serve, cut the steaks into thin slices and place on a platter or in a chaffing dish. Pour the wine-mushroom sauce over the steak. Serve with small plates and forks or wooden picks.

WINE PAIRING: *Challenger Ridge Cabernet Sauvignon*

A classic, velvety cabernet with bold flavors, this wine is balanced with hints of cherry and currants, and a long, full finish.

Q: What is the ideal size of a wine glass?

A: For red wines, your glass should hold a minimum of 12 ounces and a maximum of 16 to 24 ounces. For white wines, the glass should hold a minimum of 10 to 12 ounces.

Tenderloin Bruschetta with Horseradish and Blue Cheese

Bergevin Lane Vineyards | Walla Walla, Washington

Makes 20 appetizer servings

- 1 artisan baguette, cut on the diagonal into 20 slices (about ½-inch thick)
- ¾ to 1 pound beef tenderloin, trimmed
- Salt and freshly ground black pepper
- ⅓ cup crumbled Point Reyes blue cheese or other blue cheese
- 2 tablespoons prepared horseradish (store-bought or homemade)
- 2 tablespoons cream cheese, softened
- 1 tablespoon Extra-virgin olive oil
- 1 tablespoon finely chopped chives or green onions
- Roasted red peppers (from a small jar), cut into 20 thin strips
- ⅓ cup Balsamic Reduction (recipe follows)

Preheat the grill to high on one side (leave the other side off).

Grill the baguette slices until golden brown, about 1 minute per side. Set aside and keep warm.

Season the tenderloin with salt and pepper. Tie the tenderloin with string if necessary to ensure the same thickness throughout. Grill the beef over high heat until browned on both sides, about 3 to 4 minutes on each side. Move the tenderloin to the cool side of grill to finish cooking, for about 25 minutes. Cook until an internal meat thermometer reads 125 degrees F. Remove from the grill, tent with aluminum foil, and let rest for 10 minutes. Thinly slice the meat.

In a small mixing bowl, using a fork, blend the Point Reyes blue cheese, horse-radish, cream cheese, and olive oil. Stir in the chives and season with pepper to taste.

To serve, arrange the baguette slices on a platter. Spread a generous amount of the blue cheese–horseradish sauce on each baguette slice. Top each with a slice of tenderloin and a strip of roasted red pepper. Drizzle with a small amount of the Balsamic Reduction. Scatter chopped chives or green onions over the platter, if desired.

COOK'S NOTE: The beef tenderloin can be prepared one day in advance. Let it cool before refrigerating. Reheat slices of tenderloin for 10 minutes at 350 degrees F before placing on baguette slices. The blue cheese–horseradish mixture can also be made in advance and refrigerated.

Balsamic Reduction

1 cup balsamic vinegar

In a small saucepan, heat the balsamic vinegar over medium heat, stirring occasionally, for about 40 minutes or until reduced to ⅓ cup.

....

WINE PAIRING: *Bergevin Lane Cabernet Sauvignon, Columbia Valley*
Smooth and round, this cabernet displays earth notes, spice box, black currants, and blackberry on the palate. Subtle flavors of roasted red pepper and smoke lead to a lingering finish with a hint of sweet oak.

BERGEVIN LANE VINEYARDS

The Bergevin family settled in the Walla Walla Valley in the mid-1800s. When Annette Bergevin decided to start a winery, she looked to her roots and moved back to Walla Walla from California. She and Amber Lane partnered with her father, Gary Bergevin, who had decades of experience in the wine industry. Together, the three created Bergevin Lane Vineyards, which opened in 2003 near downtown Walla Walla.

For a period of time Bergevin Lane shared its ample space with Long Shadows Vintners, until that winery could build its own facility. Now it runs a custom-crush operation, in which its facility is used for producing wine for other wineries—all in addition to making its more than seven thousand cases of reds and whites. The wines are made by Steffan Jorgensen, who learned his craft in France, Chile, and California, before landing in Washington.

Bergevin Lane first gained a following with its "Calico" blends (one red blend and one white blend). It has since expanded into Merlots, Cabernet, Syrahs, Viogniers, and Rosés, all of which are consistently delicious, balanced, and age-worthy. The top wine is a Bordeaux-style blend called Intuition, which is Bergevin Lane's biggest, most expensive, and most cellar-worthy wine. The folks at Bergevin Lane are a fun bunch, and they obviously enjoy life. The wines, too, reveal the less-stuffy side of the industry with their youthful approachfulness, although they are seriously delicious.

Prawns and Mango Salsa Cocktail

Mercer Estates | Prosser, Washington

Makes 12 appetizer servings

  1 pound large gulf prawns (about 12), peeled and deveined

  2 tablespoons extra virgin olive oil

  2 cloves garlic, chopped

  1 teaspoon red chile flakes

  2 cups mixed salad greens, washed and patted dry

  Mango Salsa (recipe follows)

Preheat the grill to medium-high heat.

Lightly brush the grate with olive oil. In a small bowl, mix together the olive oil, garlic, and red chile flakes. Cover with plastic wrap and marinate the prawns in the mixture for 10 to 15 minutes.

Grill the prawns for 2 to 3 minutes per side, or until opaque. Fill twelve 3-ounce double-shot glasses half full with the mixed salad greens. Top with a heaping tablespoon of Mango Salsa and a grilled prawn. Serve with small forks.

Mango Salsa

  1½ tablespoons Extra-virgin olive oil

  3 tablespoons honey

  2 small ripe mangos, peeled and diced

  3 tablespoons chopped red onion

  1 large or 2 small jalapeños, finely chopped

  3 tablespoons chopped fresh cilantro

  Salt and freshly ground black pepper

In a small bowl, mix together the olive oil, honey, mango, red onion, jalapeño, and cilantro. Season with salt and pepper to taste.

RECIPE CONTRIBUTED BY CHEF FRANK MAGAÑA

. . . .

WINE PAIRING: *Mercer Estates Riesling*

This wine is brisk, tangy, and refreshing, with flavors and aromas of apricot, peach, and tangerine. With lively acidity and a little less than a percent and a half residual sugar, this Riesling lends itself nicely to food pairings.

MERCER ESTATES

One of Washington's newest producers includes some of its most savvy wine people. Back in the early 1980s, the Hogue family decided to open a little winery. It grew through the years until the several-hundred-thousand-case producer was sold to the world's largest wine company in 2001. Mike Hogue, one of two brothers who ran Hogue Cellars, stayed out of the business for five years (as was stipulated in his contract), but he began to make plans. He knew he could no longer use his name, so he turned to the Mercer family, which has been in and out of the Washington wine industry for decades. They planted Mercer Ranch Vineyards, now the famous Champoux Vineyards, in the Horse Heaven Hills, and they even opened a winery for a brief time.

With Hogue and the Mercers as partners, Mercer Estates was launched in 2007. The winery is just down the road from—and within site of—Hogue Cellars. Mercer Estates quickly hired David Forsyth, who was Hogue Cellars' director of winemaking, and secured estate grapes from some of the finest locations in the Columbia Valley. The result has been near-instant success, with production planned in the sixty-five-thousand-case range. Mike Hogue and Bud Mercer have also brought in their children as integral parts of the operation, ensuring the second generation will carry on the legacy of these two Washington farming families.

Portobello Mushrooms with Green Peppercorn Sauce

Hightower Cellars | Benton City, Washington

Makes 4 appetizer servings

>   2 cups reduced-sodium beef stock
>
>   1 tablespoon brined green peppercorns, rinsed and drained
>
>   ¼ cup Marsala wine
>
>   ½ cup heavy cream
>
>   1 tablespoon Extra-virgin olive oil
>
>   1 tablespoon butter, melted
>
>   4 fresh large portobello mushroom caps

Preheat the grill to medium heat.

Heat the beef stock in a small saucepan over medium heat until reduced to ½ cup, about 25 minutes. Stir in the peppercorns and continue reducing until only about 3 tablespoons of the stock remains. Pour in the Marsala and heavy cream. Continue to reduce for 5 to 10 minutes. Keep warm.

In a small bowl, whisk the olive oil and butter. Using a pastry brush, generously coat both sides of the portobello mushrooms with the olive oil–butter mixture. Grill the mushrooms stem-side down for 6 minutes. Turn over and grill the tops for 4 to 6 minutes longer, or until tender and nicely browned.

To serve, slice the mushrooms. Divide between four plates. Pour the Marsala-peppercorn sauce over mushrooms.

WINE PAIRING: *Hightower Cellars Cabernet Sauvignon*

This well-balanced wine expresses balance and velvetiness on the palate, right through the long, smooth finish. Red Mountain mineral aromas can be detected along with intense aromas of dark fruit, sweet spice, and a faint hint of characteristic Cabernet Sauvignon menthol.

> **Q:** Why is wine stored horizontally?
>
> **A:** It's important to store wine horizontally so that the wine stays in contact with the cork and keeps the cork moist, preventing oxidization.

Grilled Asparagus with Walla Walla Sweet Spring Onions

Yellow Hawk Cellar | Walla Walla, Washington

Makes 6 appetizer servings

    ¼ cup olive oil

    2 tablespoons balsamic vinegar

    2 tablespoons rice wine vinegar

    2 tablespoons soy sauce

    1 clove garlic, minced

    1½ pounds fresh medium-thick asparagus spears, trimmed

    6 Walla Walla spring onions with green tops attached
    (bulbs 1 to 2 inches in diameter)

    Salt and freshly ground black pepper

    Toasted sesame seeds

In a resealable 1-gallon plastic bag, mix the olive oil, balsamic vinegar, rice wine vinegar, soy sauce, and garlic. Trim green onion tops to 4 inches above bulb. Cut larger onions in half, lengthwise. Put the asparagus and onions in the marinade. Refrigerate for at least 1 hour but no longer than 4 hours (or the colors will fade).

Preheat the grill to medium heat.

Grill the asparagus and onions for 9 to 12 minutes, turning several times, until softened but not limp (brush with marinade if dry). Remove from the grill and let cool slightly.

Serve warm on small plates. Season to taste with salt and pepper. Sprinkle with toasted sesame seeds.

COOK'S NOTE: Small Walla Walla spring onions with edible green tops still attached are available in early summer. These small onions are the early form of the larger Walla Walla onions that are available June through September.

....

WINE PAIRING: *Yellow Hawk Cellar Barbera, Columbia Valley*
This 100 percent Barbera with spiced dark cherry, dark sweet chocolate, hints of green pepper, and a touch of light vanilla shows some assertive natural acidity and a medium-bodied gentle finish. Pair with all things Italian, soft cheeses, and grilled vegetables and meat.

> **Q:** What is the purpose of the indentation at the bottom of a wine bottle?
>
> **A:** The indentation strengthens the structure of the bottle and traps the sediments in the wine.

Masa with White Beans, Pancetta, and Arugula

Hedges Family Estate Winery | Benton City, Washington

Makes 6 appetizer servings

2 cups instant masa harina

1 cup water

2 tablespoons rice wine vinegar

¼ teaspoon sea salt

Freshly ground black pepper

4 ounces pancetta, chopped

6 cups fresh arugula, washed and patted dry

2 tablespoons butter

¼ cup finely chopped sweet Walla Walla onion

One 15-ounce can white beans, rinsed and drained

6 to 8 drops hot pepper sauce

1 tablespoon chopped fresh sage

Extra virgin olive oil

To make the dough, mix the instant masa harina, water, rice vinegar, salt, and pepper to taste in a medium bowl until the dough can be formed into a ball. The dough should be moist and soft but should not stick to your hands. If the dough is too dry, moisten your hands with water and work the dough until it reaches the desired consistency. Roll the dough into twelve balls a little smaller than golf balls. To form the patties, cover each ball with plastic wrap and press into a 3-inch round using the palm of your hand or the bottom of a glass. Cover the patties with plastic wrap to prevent drying out. Set aside.

In a medium skillet, cook the pancetta over medium heat until crisp, about 8 to 10 minutes. Transfer the pancetta to a paper towel to drain. Toss the arugula in the hot skillet with the pancetta fat and cook until just wilted, about a minute. Transfer the arugula to a paper towel and set aside.

In a medium saucepan, melt the butter over medium heat. Cook and stir the onions until they start to turn golden brown, about 3 minutes. Add the white beans, hot pepper sauce, and salt and pepper to taste. Cook the mixture, stirring occasionally, until the beans are almost dry and begin to hold together, about 10 minutes. Stir in the sage and pancetta.

To grill the masa patties, allow 5 minutes for the grill to heat to medium. Using a pastry brush, coat each side of the masa patties with olive oil. Grill about 3 minutes on each side or until hot.

To serve, place a heaping tablespoon of the bean-pancetta mixture in the center of each masa patty and top with the wilted arugula. Garnish with chopped basil or sage if desired.

RECIPE CONTRIBUTED BY SABRINA GREEVER

....

WINE PAIRING: *Hedges Family Estate Three Vineyards*
This classic Red Mountain wine is a blend of Cabernet Sauvignon and Merlot that oozes with dark, luscious berry and plum flavors. It shows a deep, dense color, firm yet supple tannins, and a well-defined acidity.

Prosciutto-Wrapped Grilled Shrimp

Phelps Creek Vineyard | Hood River, Oregon

Makes 16 to 20 skewers

> 2 tablespoons extra virgin olive oil
>
> Juice of 1 orange (about 3 to 4 tablespoons), plus grated zest
>
> 1 clove garlic, minced
>
> 1 teaspoon fennel seed, toasted and crushed
>
> 1 teaspoon kosher salt
>
> ½ teaspoon freshly ground black pepper
>
> 1 pound large shrimp (about 16 to 20), peeled and deveined
>
> 4 large slices prosciutto, cut into 1-inch strips
>
> 16 to 20 bamboo skewers

In a large resealable plastic bag or a glass dish, whisk the olive oil, orange juice, orange zest, garlic, fennel seed, salt, and pepper. Marinate the shrimp in the mixture for 1 to 3 hours in the refrigerator.

Soak the bamboo skewers in water for 30 minutes before grilling.

Remove the shrimp from the marinade and wrap each shrimp with a strip of prosciutto. Thread the prosciutto-wrapped shrimp on the skewers.

Preheat the grill to medium heat.

Lightly brush the grate (or a grill basket) with olive oil. Grill the shrimp about 3 minutes on each side, or until the flesh is pink, opaque, and firm. Serve immediately.

WINE PAIRING: *Phelps Creek "Unoaked" Chardonnay, Columbia Gorge*

This Chardonnay is made in stainless-steel tanks to produce a clean, crisp, refreshing wine. Bright ripe melon, orchard pear, and citrus flavors are followed by a hint of herbs and toast. Wonderful acid structure makes this perfect for pairing with a wide range of foods.

PHELPS CREEK VINEYARD

The Columbia Gorge appellation is a fascinating grape-growing region that spans the Columbia River into Oregon and Washington, around the city of Hood River to the south and Bingen and White Salmon to the north. The region ranges from dry and warm on its eastern border to cooler and wetter on the western side. Long before the area gained federal status as an official appellation, Bob Morus arrived. The international airplane pilot planted his estate vineyard near Hood River with Pinot Noir and Chardonnay.

Helping to ensure the winery's success is Rich Cushman, who has crafted wines from Oregon and Washington grapes for the better part of two decades. Cushman, who produces wines for his own label, Viento, is known for his deft touch with a wide variety of grapes. The wines for Phelps Creek range from suave Pinot Noirs to sweet dessert wines, as well as a dry Rosé. Cushman crafts no fewer than three styles of Pinot Noir, two Chardonnays, a Gewürztraminer, and even a rare cool-climate Merlot from famed Celilo Vineyards across the river in Washington.

Compared with many wines in Oregon, Phelps Creek's offerings are modestly priced, and they are especially good values when one takes into consideration their high quality. The Hood River area is well known for its abundant fruit and is quickly turning into a wine destination. Phelps Creek is well worth including on your next tour of the area.

Raspberry Glazed Pork Bites

Kyra Wines | Moses Lake, Washington

Makes 6 skewers

  ½ cup prepared raspberry jam (store-bought or homemade)

  2 teaspoons balsamic vinegar

  1 teaspoon chopped fresh rosemary

  ¼ teaspoon ground cinnamon

  3 boneless pork chops (about 4 ounces each), cut into 1-inch cubes

  Salt and freshly ground black pepper

  6 bamboo skewers

Preheat the grill to medium-high heat.

Lightly brush the grill rack with oil. Soak the bamboo skewers in water for 30 minutes before grilling.

To prepare the rosemary-raspberry glaze, heat the raspberry jam, balsamic vinegar, rosemary, and cinnamon in a small saucepan over medium heat, until melted.

Slide four or five pork cubes onto each skewer, leaving about ¼-inch space between the pieces. Season lightly with salt and pepper. Grill the skewers for 6 to 7 minutes, turning frequently, until golden and cooked through.

Turn off the grill heat. While the skewers are still on the grill, brush all sides of the pork generously with the glaze. Let the skewers sit 2 to 3 minutes before serving. Serve any remaining glaze on the side as a dipping sauce if desired.

....

WINE PAIRING: *Kyra Pinot Noir*
Enjoy flavors of red and black cherry with lots of sweet toast. Fruits of plum, sweet raspberry, and cherry pie are paired with notes of rosemary and sage.

Spot Prawn Kabobs
with Black Currant Chutney

Elephant Island Orchard Wines | Naramata, British Columbia

Makes 12 skewers

¼ cup soy sauce

¼ cup Elephant Island Black Currant Wine or other berry wine

¼ cup vegetable oil

1 teaspoon ground ginger

2 cloves garlic, chopped

24 large spot prawns (about 2 pounds), peeled and deveined

4 green onions, cut into thirds

1 ripe peach, peeled and cut into 12 chunks

Prepared black currant or other fruit chutney (store-bought or homemade), for dipping

12 bamboo skewers

Preheat the grill to medium heat.

Soak the bamboo skewers in water for 30 minutes before grilling.

In a medium bowl, whisk together the soy sauce, wine, vegetable oil, ginger, and garlic. Add the prawns, cover with plastic wrap, and marinate for 30 minutes in the refrigerator.

Thread the skewers with two prawns, a piece of green onion, and a chunk of peach. Grill for 3 to 4 minutes, turning once.

Serve with the black currant chutney.

WINE PAIRING: *Elephant Island Black Currant Wine*

Huge flavors of berry, bell pepper, and pomegranate dominate this wine, backed by the singular crispness of black currant. Serve well chilled.

ELEPHANT ISLAND ORCHARD WINES

A potential reaction that many have when encountering a fruit winery is to smile and plan to not take the products too seriously. Don't make such a mistake with Elephant Island Orchard Wines in British Columbia's Okanagan Valley. Del and Miranda Halladay launched their operation in 1999. Their goal was to make the finest and most elegant fruit wines anywhere. They take their task seriously, hand-sorting various fruits from estate and nearby orchards on the Naramata Bench. The Halladays craft wines from apples, pears, cherries, black currants, peaches, and raspberries. They even produce a rare ice wine from frozen Fuji apples. The wines range from bone dry to extremely sweet, and they pair extremely well with a wide variety of dishes.

By the way, there is no Elephant Island in nearby Okanagan Lake. In fact, the name comes from the orchard's early history. Miranda's grandparents purchased the land in the early 1970s as an investment. Grandma wanted to plant an orchard, which Grandpa thought was a "white elephant." Grandma's aesthetic—or eye for detail—won out, thus the name Elephant Island (or eye-land).

The tasting room is open seasonally and well worth a stop along the wine trail of the Naramata Bench. Those wanting to stay in the region should consider staying at The Tree House, an on-site bed-and-breakfast with a spectacular view of Okanagan Lake and the surrounding valley.

Grilled Coconut Curry Ceviche

Wooldridge Creek Vineyard and Winery | Grants Pass, Oregon

Makes 6 small plate servings

½ pound medium-large shrimp (about 8), peeled and deveined

½ pound large sea scallops

½ pound white fish (tilapia, mahi-mahi, cod)

Juice of 3 limes (about ½ cup), plus grated zest

Juice of 1 lemon (about 3 tablespoons), plus grated zest

Juice of ½ orange (about ¼ cup), plus grated zest

¼ cup extra virgin olive oil

1 medium ripe avocado, peeled and chopped

½ large red onion, finely chopped

½ cup finely chopped fresh flat leaf parsley

¼ teaspoon green curry paste

½ cup coconut milk

Salt

Preheat the grill to medium-high heat.

Lightly brush the rack with olive oil. Grill the shrimp, sea scallops, and white fish for 5 to 8 minutes, turning once. The seafood is done when the scallops become opaque, the shrimp turns pink, and the fish flakes with a fork. Remove from the grill and let cool slightly before chopping into ¼-inch pieces. Set aside.

In a medium bowl, whisk together the lime juice, lime zest, lemon juice, lemon zest, orange juice, orange zest, olive oil, avocado, red onion, and parsley. In a small bowl, stir together the green curry paste and coconut milk; pour into the avocado mixture. Gently stir in the reserved chopped seafood. Season with salt to taste. Cover and refrigerate for at least 1 hour before serving. Serve on individual plates over salad greens or on a platter with tortilla chips, if desired.

WINE PAIRING: *Wooldridge Creek Pinot Noir Rosé*

This dry Pinot Noir Rosé has notes of strawberry, watermelon, and citrus with lovely floral aromas. It is well balanced, with light acidity and a refreshing finish.

WOOLDRIDGE CREEK VINEYARD AND WINERY

Far off the beaten path—so deep into the Applegate Valley that you're closer to Napa than you are to Portland—is one of Oregon's wonderful little undiscovered wine gems. Ted and Mary Warrick purchased land for their vineyard in the mid-1970s with the idea of escaping Southern California and seeking a life-altering change in profession and scenery. Over the next quarter-century, the Warricks planted grapes generally unknown in Oregon, including Cabernet Sauvignon, Zinfandel, Tempranillo, Sangiovese, Cabernet Franc, and Petit Verdot as well as Pinot Noir.

In 2002, Greg Paneitz and Kara Olmo decided to explore Southern Oregon as a place to make wine after spending time in the French and Californian wine industries. The young couple met the Warricks, and the four saw wonderful possibilities with launching a winery. Thus Wooldridge Creek Vineyard and Winery was born.

While Wooldridge Creek is in the warmer southern climes of Oregon, it also is in an area that allows grapes to slowly ripen. Thus, Cabernet Sauvignon often doesn't come into the winery until as late as early November. The resulting wines are beautifully balanced and often much lower in alcohol than what has become typical in the American wine industry. Wooldridge Creek's wines are perfect for aging or pairing with food and should be highly sought-after.

Blackberry Chipotle Sockeye Salmon

Woodinville Wine Cellars | Woodinville, Washington

Makes 4 small plate servings

> 4 fillets sockeye salmon (about 4 to 5 ounces each)
>
> Blackberry Chipotle Sauce (recipe follows)

Preheat the grill to medium heat.

Lightly brush the grill rack with oil. Grill the salmon fillets for 8 to 10 minutes, turning once, until the fish flakes easily with a fork.

To serve, place the salmon fillets on four plates and spoon the Blackberry Chipotle Sauce on top. Garnish with a sprig of fresh thyme if desired.

Blackberry Chipotle Sauce

> 1 teaspoon extra virgin olive oil
>
> 1 tablespoon finely chopped shallots
>
> 1/8 teaspoon chipotle powder
>
> 1/4 teaspoon dried thyme leaves
>
> 1 cup Woodinville Wine Cellars Little Bear Creek Red Wine
> or other dry red wine
>
> 1/8 teaspoon sea salt
>
> 1 tablespoon sugar
>
> 1 cup fresh or frozen blackberries, divided

Heat the olive oil for a few minutes in small saucepan over medium heat. Stir in the shallots, chipotle powder, and thyme. Cook until the shallots are translucent, about 2 to 3 minutes, stirring frequently. Add the wine, sea salt, sugar, and 1/2 cup of the blackberries. Simmer uncovered and reduce the liquid to a 1/3 cup, about 20 minutes, stirring frequently.

Remove the mixture from the heat and stir in the remaining blackberries. Serve immediately.

COOK'S NOTE: You may prepare the Blackberry Chipotle Sauce up to 4 hours ahead. Just reheat over low heat and add berries.

....

WINE PAIRING: *Woodinville Wine Cellars Little Bear Creek Red Wine*
This blend of five Bordeaux varietals includes Merlot, Cabernet Sauvignon, Cabernet Franc, Malbec, and Petite Verdot. Dry on the palate with notes of violets, pepper, and black fruit.

Q: What does "AVA" refer to?

A: American Viticultural Areas (AVAs) are official grape-growing regions defined by soil, climate, and geographic features that set them apart from the surrounding area.

Grilled Salmon with Hazelnut–Brown Butter Sauce

Torii Mor Winery | Dundee, Oregon

Makes 8 small plate servings

> 2½ to 3 pounds salmon fillet
>
> Salt and freshly ground black pepper
>
> 2 tablespoons extra virgin olive oil
>
> ¼ cup white wine
>
> 4 tablespoons fresh lemon juice, divided
>
> ½ cup (1 stick) butter
>
> ⅓ cup coarsely chopped roasted hazelnuts

Preheat the grill to medium-high heat.

Place salmon, skin side down, on a large piece of heavy-duty aluminum foil. Curl up the sides of the foil slightly to catch juices. Sprinkle with salt and pepper. Drizzle the olive oil, wine, and 2 tablespoons of the lemon juice evenly over the salmon. Cook, with the grill lid closed, until the salmon is just opaque in the center, about 10 to 15 minutes.

Meanwhile, melt the butter in a skillet over medium-high heat. Cook, stirring occasionally, until the butter browns and begins to have a nutty aroma, about 5 minutes. Remove from heat and stir in the hazelnuts and the remaining lemon juice. Season to taste with salt and pepper.

Transfer the fillet of salmon to a large platter. Pour the hazelnut–brown butter sauce over the cooked salmon. Serve on individual plates, garnished with a slice of lemon if desired.

RECIPE CONTRIBUTED BY ARIANA SHERLOCK

WINE PAIRING: *Torii Mor Oregon Pinot Noir*

A soft, silky mouthfeel is enhanced with flavors of ripe, juicy fruit, with expressions of cocoa, prunes, barrel toast, and earth layers coming forward with age. The finish is wonderfully balanced and lingers with long notes of berry fruit.

TORII MOR WINERY

In 1993, Donald Olson launched this small, high-end winery in Oregon's Dundee Hills with the intent of focusing on super-premium Pinot Noir. Olson also purchased McDaniel Vineyard, a property planted in 1972, making it one of the Willamette Valley's oldest vineyards. Olson got off to a great start with Patty Green and Jim Anderson, two highly talented winemakers who quickly put Torii Mor on the Oregon wine map, making its Pinot Noirs highly sought-after. When the pair left to launch Patricia Green Cellars in 2000, famed winemaker Joe Dobbes stepped in to craft Torii Mor's Pinot Noirs for a couple of vintages. Today, Jacque Tardy, a Burgundian by birth, makes the wines.

The fanciful name, Torii Mor, is one that Olson came up with by combining words from two languages: "Torii" is Japanese for the ornate gates that guard the entrance to gardens, and "Mor" is an ancient Scandinavian word for earth. Olson figures that Pinot Noir is a beautiful gateway to the earth. Through Torii Mor's years in the Oregon wine industry, it certainly has lived up to that reputation.

Today, Torii Mor has branched out to include such wines as Chardonnay, Pinot Gris, Pinot Blanc, Viognier, and Gewürztraminer. Its focus continues to remain on Pinot Noir, though, as it crafts no fewer than nine styles of the noble variety.

Lamb Skewers with Yogurt Cucumber Dipping Sauce

Tapteil Vineyard Winery | Benton City, Washington

Makes 12 skewers

 ¼ cup lemon agrumato olive oil or extra virgin olive oil

 Juice of 1 lemon (about 3 tablespoons)

 1 tablespoon minced garlic

 6 sprigs of fresh rosemary, leaves chopped

 15 to 20 fresh mint leaves, chopped

 Salt and freshly ground black pepper

 1½ pounds trimmed boneless leg of lamb, cut into 1-inch cubes

 12 rosemary branches (to use as skewers), if desired, or 12 bamboo skewers

 Yogurt Cucumber Dipping Sauce (recipe follows)

Soak the rosemary branch skewers or bamboo skewers in water for 30 minutes before grilling.

Mix together the lemon agrumato olive oil, lemon juice, garlic, rosemary, mint, salt, and pepper in a resealable 1-gallon plastic bag. Shake well. Add the lamb cubes and shake to coat with the marinade. Marinate the lamb at room temperature while assembling the Yogurt Cucumber Dipping Sauce.

Preheat the grill to medium-high heat.

While the grill heats, place four to five marinated lamb cubes on each skewer. Grill the skewers, rotating them, until nicely brown but not overcooked, about 8 minutes for medium rare. These will cook quickly, so watch them carefully.

Serve the skewers with the dipping sauce and warm pita bread, if desired.

Yogurt Cucumber Dipping Sauce

    1 pint Greek-style yogurt

    2 tablespoons fresh lemon juice

    2 teaspoons crushed garlic

    1 tablespoon finely chopped fresh mint

    1 tablespoon finely chopped fresh parsley

    1 cup diced English cucumber

    Salt and freshly ground black pepper

In a medium serving bowl, mix together the yogurt, lemon juice, garlic, mint, parsley, and cucumber. Season with salt and pepper to taste.

....

WINE PAIRING: *Tapteil Cabernet Sauvignon, Red Mountain*
An extraordinary violet nose leads to deep flavors of dark cherries, chocolate, and spice that fill the palate. The rich chewy finish lingers lavishly.

Herbed Lamb Chops with Syrah Reduction

Trust Cellars | Walla Walla, Washington

Makes 6 appetizer servings

> 2 tablespoons extra virgin olive oil
>
> 1 clove garlic, minced
>
> 1 tablespoon finely chopped fresh rosemary
>
> 1 tablespoon finely chopped fresh Italian parsley
>
> ½ tablespoon chopped fresh thyme leaves
>
> ½ tablespoon coarsely crushed fennel seed
>
> ¼ teaspoon salt
>
> ¼ teaspoon freshly ground black pepper
>
> 6 baby lamb rib chops (about 1 ¼ pounds), bones frenched
>
> Syrah Reduction (recipe follows)

In a shallow bowl, mix together the olive oil, garlic, rosemary, parsley, thyme, fennel seed, salt, and pepper. Cut the lamb rack into single chops and coat the lamb chops completely with the herb mixture. Cover and refrigerate 1 to 2 hours.

Preheat the grill to medium-high heat.

Grill the lamb chops about 4 minutes per side for medium-rare. Serve immediately with the Syrah Reduction as a dipping sauce.

COOK'S NOTE: "Frenching the bones" is a process whereby the excess fat is removed from the lamb bones to clean them up before cooking. This is something you can ask your butcher to do for you.

Syrah Reduction

½ cup Trust Cellars Syrah or other dry red wine

1 small shallot, finely chopped

¼ cup (½ stick) cold butter, cut into small pieces

Salt and freshly ground black pepper

Heat the wine and shallot in a small saucepan over medium-high heat. Simmer uncovered until reduced by one half, then turn the heat to low. Stir in the butter, a few pieces at a time, whisking to incorporate each addition before adding more. Season to taste with salt and pepper.

....

WINE PAIRING: *Trust Cellars Syrah*

This wine has aromas of white pepper, blackberries, plum, cherry pie, and a hint of eucalyptus.

Smoky Flat Iron Steak Bites with Chimichurri Sauce

Sweet Valley Wines | Walla Walla, Washington

Makes 8 appetizer servings

> 2 flat iron steaks (about 10 ounces each and ¾-inch thick)
>
> ¼ cup white balsamic vinegar
>
> 1 tablespoon butter, melted
>
> Smoked sea salt and smoked black pepper
>
> 8 wooden skewers
>
> Chimichurri Sauce (recipe follows)

Put the steaks in a plastic bag. Pour in the white balsamic vinegar and marinate in the refrigerator for 4 hours or overnight.

Preheat the grill to medium-high heat.

Remove the steaks from the marinade. Using a pastry brush, coat both sides of the steaks with the butter. Sprinkle with salt and pepper. Grill steaks, turning once, until nicely charred and medium-rare, about 8 minutes. Transfer the steaks to a platter and let rest for 10 minutes.

Cut the steak into ½-inch-thick slices. Weave the steak bites onto the skewers and arrange them on a platter. Spoon some Chimichurri Sauce over the skewers, sprinkle with a little more salt, if desired. Place the remaining sauce in a bowl for dipping.

Chimichurri Sauce

½ cup extra virgin olive oil

2 tablespoons white balsamic vinegar

¼ cup chopped fresh parsley

¼ cup chopped fresh cilantro

2 piquillo peppers or roasted red bell peppers (from a jar), rinsed, drained, and chopped

2 cloves garlic, minced

1 tablespoon minced Walla Walla sweet onion

½ tablespoon fresh lime juice

1 tablespoon crushed red pepper

Salt and freshly ground black pepper

In a medium bowl, whisk together the olive oil and white balsamic vinegar. Stir in the parsley, cilantro, piquillo peppers, garlic, onion, lime juice, and crushed red pepper. Season to taste with salt and pepper and let stand for at least 20 minutes before serving.

COOK'S NOTE: The Chimichurri Sauce can be made ahead and refrigerated for up to two days in an airtight container. Bring to room temperature before serving.

....

WINE PAIRING: *Sweet Valley Syrah*
Spice flavors intertwine with berry notes to create a pleasing palate, while smooth, earthy, fruit tones greet the nose with a hint of clove.

Grilled Oysters with Cranberry Salsa

Westport Winery | Aberdeen, Washington

Makes 12 appetizer servings

> 12 oysters in the shell, rinsed
>
> Cranberry Salsa (recipe follows)

Preheat the grill to high heat.

Cover the grill with pierced aluminum foil and scatter the oysters over the foil. Close the grill for 5 to 6 minutes, or until the shells open and the oysters are thoroughly cooked (discard any that do not open).

Remove oysters from the grill, top with Cranberry Salsa, and serve immediately.

Cranberry Salsa

> One 12-ounce bag cranberries, fresh or frozen
>
> 1 bunch cilantro, washed, patted dry, and chopped
>
> ¼ medium red onion, chopped
>
> 1 pickled jalapeño, chopped
>
> 1 tablespoon fresh lime juice
>
> ¾ cup sugar
>
> Dash of sea salt

Put the cranberries, cilantro, red onion, jalapeño, lime juice, sugar, and salt in a food processor and pulse until lightly chopped and blended. Refrigerate at least 30 minutes (or up to 2 hours) before serving with freshly grilled oysters.

....

WINE PAIRING: *Westport Winery's Shorebird Chardonnay*
This dry stainless-steel–aged Chardonnay is fruit-forward with hints of citrus and melon. A mineral backbone provides structure and balance.

Grilled Asparagus Chèvre Tartines

Gård Vintners | Royal City, Washington

Makes 12 appetizer servings

> 12 spears fresh asparagus, trimmed
>
> Extra-virgin olive oil
>
> Sea salt and freshly ground black pepper
>
> 1 crusty baguette, cut on the diagonal into 12 slices (about ½-inch thick and 4 to 6 inches long)
>
> 1 clove garlic, halved
>
> 8 ounces fresh goat cheese (chèvre), softened

Preheat the grill to high heat.

In a medium bowl, generously coat the asparagus with olive oil and season to taste with sea salt and pepper. Using a pastry brush, coat both sides of the baguette slices with olive oil.

Grill the asparagus until slightly charred on all sides, about 5 minutes (roll a quarter turn every minute or so). At the same time, grill the baguette slices, charring only the edges, about 15 seconds on each side.

Immediately remove the asparagus and the bread from the grill. Rub each baguette slice with garlic in one smooth swipe. Spread a generous portion of the goat cheese on each baguette slice while still warm.

Slice the grilled asparagus on the diagonal into long strips. Top each tartine (open-faced sandwich) with the asparagus. Season to taste with salt and pepper.

RECIPE CONTRIBUTED BY CHEF "BIG JOHN" CAUDILL

WINE PAIRING: *Gård Vintners Dry Riesling*

A completely dry style of Riesling with balanced acidity and a crisp finish, this lively fruit-forward wine has hints of melons, stone fruits, citrus, green apple, and honey.

Q: To what does the vintage date refer?

A: This is the year in which the grapes were harvested, not the year that the wine was bottled (for some wines, this happens years later).

SMALL PLATES

Moroccan Lamb Meatballs with Spiced Tomato Sauce

Pears with Blue Cheese and Walnuts

Dungeness Crab Gazpacho

Arugula and Baby Spinach Salad

Minted Crab Salad with Chilled Cucumber Water

Crab Salad Tower with Mango and Papaya

Rock Shrimp with Creamy Pesto Dressing

Squash Napoleon with Parmesan Crisp and White Peach Sauce

Roasted Vegetable and Shrimp Orzo

Ravioli with Linguiça Sausage and Tomato Coulis

Flatbread with Caramelized Onions and Butternut Squash

Buffalo-Style Flatbread Pizza

Spicy Chicken Pita

Ginger Mussels

Seared Beef Tenderloin and Stilton Tartines

Manchego Polenta with Spicy Shrimp

Pan-Seared Halibut with Quinoa and Corn Salad

Lamb with Morel Mushroom Sauce and Parmesan Polenta

Spinach and Feta Phyllo Squares

Kahlúa Prawns with Lemon Buerre Blanc Sauce

Dungeness Crab with Lemon-Sorrel Aioli

Seared Scallops Provençal

Sea Stacks with Bell Pepper Sauce

Burton Seared Ahi with Citrus Coulis

Wild Game with Blueberry Compote

Blueberry Braised Short Ribs with Blue Cheese Polenta Cake

New York Steak Strips with Mushroom and Sun-Dried Tomatoes

Fusilli Pasta with Brie and Sun-Dried Tomatoes

Pesto-Scallop Pouches

Moroccan Lamb Meatballs with Spiced Tomato Sauce

Weisinger's of Ashland | Ashland, Oregon

Makes 6 small plate servings

> 1 ¼ pounds ground lamb
>
> Moroccan Spice Blend (available at specialty food stores)
>
> 1 egg, beaten
>
> ¼ cup ketchup
>
> ½ tablespoon ground cumin
>
> ½ tablespoon ground coriander
>
> 1 tablespoon extra virgin olive oil
>
> ¼ cup minced yellow onion
>
> ½ tablespoon minced garlic
>
> ½ tablespoon minced shallots
>
> 1 cinnamon stick
>
> 2 cups tomato purée
>
> ½ cup vegetable or chicken stock
>
> 1 tablespoon thinly sliced fresh mint
>
> 1 tablespoon minced fresh Italian parsley
>
> Salt and freshly ground black pepper

Preheat the oven to 350 degrees F.

In a large bowl, mix together the ground lamb, Moroccan Spice Blend, egg, and ketchup, being careful not to overwork the meat. Form into 1¼-ounce balls, about the size of a ping-pong ball. Place the meatballs on a large baking sheet. Put in the oven and bake for approximately 20 minutes, or until the meatballs are no longer pink inside.

Toast the cumin and coriander in a small, dry skillet over low heat until fragrant, about 2 minutes, stirring frequently.

In a large saucepan, heat the olive oil over medium heat. Add the onion; cook and stir until soft, about 5 minutes. Stir in the garlic, shallots, cinnamon stick, and toasted cumin-coriander blend. Cook over low heat, about 3 to 4 minutes. Stir in the tomato purée and bring to a boil. Add the vegetable stock, mint, and parsley. Season to taste with salt and pepper. Simmer uncovered for about 10 minutes. Remove the cinnamon stick. Put the meatballs in the sauce.

To serve, spoon the sauce and meatballs onto individual plates or in shallow bowls. Garnish with toasted slivered almonds and chopped fresh mint, if desired. Serve with warm pita wedges.

. . . .

WINE PAIRING: *Weisinger's of Ashland Mescolare Lot 15*
This proprietary red blend is dry and spicy, with dark fruit flavors and terrific tannins. It's a wine that benefits beautifully from decanting.

Pears with Blue Cheese and Walnuts

Bainbridge Island Vineyards and Winery | Bainbridge Island, Washington

Makes 4 small plate servings

> 2 unpeeled Comice pears, cored and chopped
>
> ⅓ cup crumbled Gorgonzola cheese
>
> ¼ cup chopped walnuts
>
> 4 teaspoons honey
>
> Grape leaves for garnish

Preheat the broiler.

Position the oven rack 5 to 6 inches from the broiler element. Place the pears in four ramekins and top evenly with the Gorgonzola and walnuts. Drizzle with the honey. Broil for 5 minutes, or until the walnuts are toasted and pears are heated through.

Place each ramekin on a fresh grape leaf and serve these small plates warm.

....

WINE PAIRING: *Bainbridge Island Winery Late Harvest Botrytised Siegerrebe*
This wine has powerful layers of mandarin, pink grapefruit, apricot, honey, and spice. Styled after the French Sauternes, but fermented from an incredibly flavorful German grape variety. Pure liquid gold!

BAINBRIDGE ISLAND VINEYARDS AND WINERY

If you want to talk about embracing a sense of place, nobody does that more in Washington than Gerard and Jo Ann Bentryn, owners of Bainbridge Island Vineyards & Winery. Just a thirty-minute ferry ride from downtown Seattle is the pastoral setting for this family operation. The Bentryns launched their winery in 1977, pioneers in the modern Washington wine industry and most certainly for cool-climate viticulture in Western Washington. They championed the Puget Sound American Viticultural Area, a wine-growing region that stretches from the Canadian border above Bellingham along the edge of the Olympic Peninsula through the islands and as far south as Olympia.

When you walk into the tasting room at the winery, expect a lecture on the virtues of growing wine grapes on Bainbridge Island, then taste those virtues when the pours begin. Don't be put off by the varieties you encounter here or at other wineries that practice viticulture in the Puget Sound appellation. Wine from such grapes as Siegerrebe, Müller-Thurgau, and Madeleine Angevine can result in perfectly delicious wines. In fact, the Bentryns are often credited with introducing Siegerrebe, an Austrian grape, to the United States. And one of the finest dessert wines you'll taste anywhere is Bainbridge Island's late-harvest, botrytis-affected Siegerrebe, an amber-colored nectar of the wine gods that should be a treasured bottle in any serious collector's cellar.

The Bentryns also make wines from island strawberries and raspberries—and they're two of the Northwest's finest fruit wines.

Dungeness Crab Gazpacho

De Ponte Cellars | Dayton, Oregon

Makes 6 appetizer servings

2½ pounds vine-ripened tomatoes, chopped

1 medium red bell pepper, chopped

½ cup peeled, seeded, and finely chopped English cucumber

¼ cup finely chopped Walla Walla sweet onion

1 fresh serrano chile, seeded, veins removed, and finely chopped

2 cloves garlic, minced

2 tablespoons red wine vinegar

½ teaspoon ground cumin

½ teaspoon salt

3 turns freshly ground black pepper

½ cup ice water

½ pound cooked Dungeness crabmeat

In a large bowl, mix together the tomatoes, red bell pepper, cucumber, onion, serrano chile, garlic, red wine vinegar, cumin, salt, pepper, and ice water. Cover and refrigerate for 1 hour.

To serve, pour the gazpacho in martini glasses and top with the crabmeat. Serve with demitasse spoons.

....

WINE PAIRING: *De Ponte Cellars DFB Estate Melon*

This dry white wine exudes green apple and pear aromas, with white peach and lemon notes and a touch of vanilla. The palate is soft and well balanced, with nice acidity on the finish.

DE PONTE CELLARS

It is easy for a young producer to get lost in the ever-more-crowded winery scene of the northern Willamette Valley. Such is not the case with De Ponte Cellars.

Scott and Rae Baldwin own this small operation in the town of Dayton, Oregon, and farm the seventeen-acre estate vineyard, which is planted to Pinot Noir and Melon. The latter is a rather rare white wine grape, known as Muscadet, or *Melon de Bourgogne* in France.

The Baldwins launched the winery in 2001, and produce wines that perfectly mirror the "terroir" of the Dundee Hills. The region's red soils are the result of ancient fractured basalt, which tends to help Pinot Noir produce wines loaded with bright red fruit aromas and flavors.

In their youth, wines from the Dundee Hills—and De Ponte Cellars in particular—provide stunning notes of cherries, raspberries, and wild strawberries.

Though De Ponte is somewhat new to the Dundee Hills, home to many of Oregon's oldest and most fabled wine producers, the vineyard is not. It is one of the oldest in the appellation. When the Baldwins took it over, the Pinot Noir vines were head-pruned, meaning they looked more like a bush than a vine. They have since retrained the vines to be more standard and easier to farm.

De Ponte is one of those bright, young producers that is destined to be known as one of the finest wineries in the region.

Arugula and Baby Spinach Salad

House of Rose Winery | Kelowna, British Columbia

Makes 6 small plate servings

    3 slices bacon

    ½ cup cubed 12-grain or sourdough bread (about 2 slices)

    1 clove garlic, minced

    6 tablespoons extra virgin olive oil

    4 tablespoons balsamic vinegar or lemon juice

    6 cups fresh arugula, washed and patted dry

    6 cups baby spinach, washed and patted dry

    12 small fresh white button mushrooms, thinly sliced

    1 medium red onion, cut into 12 thin rings

    12 fresh chives, snipped into small pieces

    One 11-ounce can mandarin orange slices, drained

    Freshly ground black pepper

In medium skillet, fry the bacon over medium-high heat until crisp. Drain on a paper towel. When the bacon has cooled, crumble into small pieces and set aside.

Turn the skillet down to medium-low and add the bread cubes and garlic to the bacon drippings. Cook, stirring frequently, until the bread is golden, about 3 minutes. Drain these croutons on paper towels and set aside.

Whisk together the olive oil and balsamic vinegar in a medium bow. Toss with the arugula and spinach.

To serve, place the greens on individual plates. Top with the mushrooms, red onion, chives, mandarin oranges, and the reserved bacon and croutons. Season to taste with pepper.

....

WINE PAIRING: *House of Rose Summer White*

This is a great all-around summer wine with a touch of sweetness and bright flavors of lemon, pineapple, and grapefruit. Serve well chilled.

Minted Crab Salad
with Chilled Cucumber Water
Mission Hill Family Estate | Okanagan, British Columbia

Makes 4 small plate servings

    2 cucumbers, peeled, seeded, and coarsely chopped

    ½ leek, diced, white part only

    ½ fennel bulb, chopped

    1 tablespoon chopped fresh dill

    ½ tablespoon sea salt

    4 ounces cooked Dungeness crabmeat

    1 tablespoon mayonnaise

    1 tablespoon thinly sliced fresh mint

    1 teaspoon grated fresh ginger

    Salt

    Fresh mint leaves

Put the cucumbers, leek, fennel, dill, and salt in a food processor and puree until smooth.

Place a large piece of cheesecloth in a strainer and set over a bowl. Pour the cucumber puree into the cheesecloth; tie together the ends of the cloth to form a bag. Allow the contents of the cheesecloth to drain into the bowl overnight in the refrigerator.

The next day, gently squeeze the bag to press out any remaining moisture. Discard the bag and its contents. Pour the cucumber water through a fine sieve.

In a small bowl, mix together the crab, mayonnaise, mint, and ginger; add salt to taste. Using a spoon or small ice cream scoop, place a mound of the crab salad on a small appetizer plate. Garnish with mint leaf, if desired. Pour cucumber water into a shot glass and serve alongside the salad. Serve immediately.

....

WINE PAIRING: *Mission Hill Reserve Riesling*
This rich, plush off-dry wine has refreshing notes of citrus fruits, apples, and melons. Its great acidity makes it a perfect match for this dish.

Crab Salad Tower with Mango and Papaya

Daedalus Cellars | Dundee, Oregon

Makes 4 small plate servings

Vegetable oil, for deep-frying

1 plantain, peeled, halved lengthwise, and cut into ⅛-inch slices

1 papaya, peeled and finely diced

1 mango, peeled and finely diced

Avocado Vinaigrette (recipe follows), divided

8 ounces cooked Dungeness crabmeat

Heat 1½ inches of vegetable oil in a medium sauté pan to 375 degrees F.

Fry the plantain slices for about 2 to 3 minutes, stirring and turning frequently, until golden brown. (They should be slightly crisp on the outside but soft on the inside.) Remove the plantain slices with a skimmer or slotted spoon and put them on paper towels to drain.

In a small bowl, gently mix together the papaya and mango with half of the Avocado Vinaigrette.

To form the "salad tower," remove the top and bottom of small fruit or vegetable can (such as an 11-ounce mandarin orange can; about 3 inches in diameter). Place the can in the middle of an individual serving plate. Spoon one-quarter of the fruit mixture into the can and top with one-quarter of the crabmeat. Press down lightly to set the ingredients. Gently slide the can up and off the salad. Rinse and dry the can before preparing the remaining towers.

To serve, drizzle the remaining half of the Avocado Vinaigrette around the tower on each plate. Scatter plantain slices around tower.

Avocado Vinaigrette

½ avocado, peeled and pitted

1 teaspoon fresh lime juice

¼ cup extra virgin olive oil

Salt

In a blender or food processor, purée the avocado, lime juice, olive oil, and salt to taste. Thin the mixture with water if necessary to achieve desired consistency. Season to taste with additional salt. Refrigerate the vinaigrette for at least 2 hours before serving.

....

WINE PAIRING: *Daedalus Cellars "Maresh Vineyard" Riesling*
A medium-bodied, intensely perfumed, vibrant white wine with crisp acidity, texture, and complexity. This pairs particularly well with seafood and light cream or citrus sauces.

Rock Shrimp with Creamy Pesto Dressing

Tildio Winery | Manson, Washington

Makes 4 small plate servings

> 1 pound rock shrimp or large shrimp (about 25), peeled and deveined
>
> Pinch of salt
>
> 1 teaspoon sugar
>
> Basil Pesto (recipe follows), divided
>
> ¼ cup mayonnaise
>
> 2 to 3 tablespoons buttermilk
>
> 6 cups baby greens, washed and patted dry
>
> 2 tablespoons toasted pine nuts

Bring a pot of water to boil and add the shrimp, salt, and sugar. Cook the shrimp until pink and cooked through, about 3 minutes. Drain and transfer the shrimp to a bowl of ice water to stop the cooking. Drain shrimp again and blot with a paper towel. Toss the shrimp with a few spoonfuls of the Basil Pesto to coat lightly, then set aside.

To make the dressing, mix the remaining pesto with the mayonnaise. Whisk in the buttermilk to thin to desired consistency (thin enough to pour).

To serve, place the shrimp on a plate of baby greens. Drizzle with the creamy pesto dressing and sprinkle with toasted pine nuts.

COOK'S NOTE: To peel rock shrimp, use a sharp kitchen scissors to snip through the back, down the middle and to the base of the tail. Gently separate shell from flesh and remove sand vein by rinsing under cold running water.

Basil Pesto

1 clove garlic, chopped

1 cup fresh basil leaves

2 tablespoons toasted pine nuts or macadamia nuts

Pinch of ground cayenne pepper

¼ cup Extra-virgin olive oil

¼ cup finely grated Parmesan cheese

Salt and freshly ground black pepper

Put the garlic, basil, pine nuts, and cayenne pepper in a food processor and pulse for a few minutes until well blended. Slowly add the olive oil while the food processor is still running. (If too thick, add a little more olive oil to thin the mixture.)

Transfer the pesto to a bowl and stir in the Parmesan. Season to taste with salt and pepper.

....

WINE PAIRING: *Tildio Sauvignon Blanc*
A crisp and bright dry Sauvignon Blanc made in a New Zealand–inspired style. This refreshing wine is loaded with tropical fruit, pink grapefruit, and a light touch of citrus.

TILDIO WINERY

Seattle native Katy Perry started her winemaking career as an intern at famed Robert Mondavi Winery in California's Napa Valley, while attending the University of California at Davis to earn enology and viticulture degrees. She spent time at Geyser Peak and Stag's Leap before returning home to Washington in 2000 for a winemaking job at Chateau Ste. Michelle.

Perry met future husband, Milum, on a ski lift in the Chelan, Washington area. After a stint as inaugural winemaker for Tsillan Cellars in Chelan, she and Milum launched Tildio, a winery and vineyard near Lake Chelan. They named it after the killdeer, a bird that happens to make its home in their area. As "killdeer" would not have been a great marketing move, the Perrys chose the Spanish name: *tildio.*

The eight-acre property was purchased in 2001, and the vineyard planting began in earnest. The winery building was finished in spring 2005, when the tasting room opened. Very quickly, Tildio established itself as one of the Chelan Valley's bright young stars. With the release of the 2003 vintage, the reds earned rave reviews from critics and consumers alike. The Perrys have not fallen into the Cabernet/Merlot/Syrah rut either, as they produce everything from Sangiovese to Zinfandel to Temprañillo, along with blends and Rosés along the way. One of their finest wines is Malbec, an often-underappreciated red Bordeaux grape. With the Chelan region exploding with tourism and winemaking, Tildio has a bright future indeed.

Squash Napoleon with Parmesan Crisp and White Peach Sauce

Tinhorn Creek Vineyards | Oliver, British Columbia

Makes 4 small plate servings

> 1½ pounds zucchini (about 2½-inches in diameter), cut into ¼-inch-thick slices
>
> Vegetable oil for brushing zucchini
>
> Parmesan Crisps (recipe follows)
>
> White Peach Sauce (recipe follows)

Using a pastry brush, coat the zucchini slices with vegetable oil. Sauté the zucchini over medium heat, about 5 minutes per side, until fork-tender. Set aside.

To assemble the napoleons, place a zucchini slice on each plate and top with a Parmesan Crisp. Repeat, making two more layers of the zucchini and the crisp.

Serve with the White Peach Sauce.

Parmesan Crisps

> 3 ounces (¾ cup) shredded Parmesan cheese

Preheat the oven to 350 degrees F.

Line a large baking sheet with parchment paper. Form 1 tablespoon of the Parmesan into a 2½-inch circle. Repeat with the remaining cheese until you have formed 12 circles. Bake for 5 minutes, or until the cheese is melted. Let cool, then remove the crisps from baking sheet.

COOK'S NOTE: The Parmesan Crisps can be made up to two days in advance and kept in a dry, airtight container.

White Peach Sauce

3 ripe white peaches

¼ cup sugar

½ cup water

2 teaspoons fresh lemon juice

2 sprigs of fresh rosemary

Pinch of salt

In a large saucepan of boiling water, blanch the peaches for 30 seconds. Drain and let cool. Peel, pit, and slice the peaches; set aside.

In the same saucepan, bring sugar and water to a boil, stirring occasionally, until the sugar dissolves. Reduce the heat and simmer the mixture uncovered for 4 minutes. Add the peach slices, lemon juice, and rosemary. Simmer uncovered for 15 to 20 minutes, or until the peaches are soft. Discard the rosemary sprigs and add the salt. In a food processor, blend the mixture until smooth. Serve warm.

RECIPE CONTRIBUTED BY MANUEL FERREIRA

....

WINE PAIRING: *Tinhorn Creek Oldfield's Collection 2Bench*
This proprietary white wine blend has a cool, crisp acidity that makes it practically sparkle on the palate. The aromas of citrus and green apple are echoed in its flavor, along with hints of lush tropical and tree fruit.

TINHORN CREEK VINEYARDS

Growing up in California's Sonoma County, Sandra Oldfield never—ever—imagined she would make wine in British Columbia. Even as she went to the University of California at Davis to learn winemaking, the thought never crossed her mind. In fact, she didn't even realize they made wine north of the border. Then she met Kenn Oldfield in one of her classes. He was from Alberta and had a dream. Ultimately, that dream included Sandra, and they launched Tinhorn Creek Vineyards in 1993 with two other partners.

The winery, just north of the border near the Okanagan Valley town of Oliver, was a first of its kind in British Columbia, as it looked straight out of California in architecture and design. Estate vineyards on both sides of the valley provide Tinhorn its grapes, and a demonstration vineyard just below the tasting room gives visitors a close-up view of the fruit. Everything is done deliberately and with a focus on class and elegance at Tinhorn. While this attitude is now more prevalent throughout the British Columbia wine industry, it started with the Oldfields. Tinhorn also built an amphitheater at the winery, where it can seat four hundred for the six or so concerts held each summer.

Tinhorn's most famous wine is their Merlot, which sells out quickly. And the Gewürztraminer, a white wine with a limited following in the United States, has a near-cult following at the winery. One famous California critic declared it the finest outside of Alsace.

Roasted Vegetable and Shrimp Orzo

Vin du Lac Winery | Chelan, Washington

Makes 6 small plate servings

　　2 medium red bell peppers, cut into ½-inch slices

　　2 medium green bell peppers, cut into ½-inch slices

　　1 medium red onion, cut into ½-inch slices

　　2½ tablespoons minced garlic

　　¼ cup plus 2 tablespoons extra virgin olive oil, divided

　　1 pound small shrimp (about 31 to 40)

　　Juice of 1 lemon (about 3 tablespoons)

　　2 cups dry orzo, cooked according to package directions
　　(about 6 cups cooked)

　　Salt and freshly ground black pepper

　　½ cup crumbled feta cheese

　　¼ cup chopped roasted hazelnuts

Preheat the oven to 350 degrees F.

Put the red and green bell peppers, onion, garlic, and ¼ cup of the olive oil in a baking pan. Mix the vegetables with a wooden spoon to coat with ¼ cup of the olive oil. Roast for 25 minutes, or until the vegetables are fork-tender. Set aside.

In a medium saucepan, bring water to boil and cook the shrimp for 2 minutes, or until pink. Drain, let cool, peel, and devein. Slice the shrimp in half lengthwise and set aside.

In a large bowl, whisk together the lemon juice and the remaining 2 tablespoons of olive oil. Add the roasted vegetables, orzo, and shrimp. Season to taste with salt and pepper and toss gently.

Divide the mixture onto six plates. Sprinkle with feta and hazelnuts.

WINE PAIRING: *Vin du Lac Les Amis*

Off-dry, rich, and aromatic, this Riesling and Muscat blend is rare indeed, but they complement each other wonderfully. The tastes are soft and creamy with just enough acid for balance. Flavor notes of honeysuckle, honey, and a hint of citrus and melon.

VIN DU LAC WINERY

Before the turn of the twenty-first century, winemaking in north-central Washington was nearly nonexistent. Today, the field is crowded, with dozens upon dozens of wineries popping up in and around Wenatchee, Leavenworth, and Chelan. Producing arguably the finest wines in the region is Vin du Lac, a winery whose name means "Wine of the Lake."

Originally known as Chelan Wine Co., the winery changed its name to distinguish itself from an ever-increasing number of producers using the name of the beautiful lake. Yet owner/winemaker Larry Lehmbecker has set himself apart from the field with some of the finest wines in the state.

His consistently greatest effort is with Cabernet Franc, a wine that stands out as one of the finest red wines around. He also crafts a wide number of other wines, ranging from Cabernet Sauvignon, to Syrah, to blends on the red side, and Viognier, Riesling, and Sauvignon Blanc for whites.

Lehmbecker and Michaela Markusson launched the winery in 2003, and Vin du Lac has quickly gained a strong following. Vin du Lac also has begun to offer a full menu of bistro-style fare during summer months. What better way to enjoy a day at Lake Chelan than with a great glass of wine and a plate of fresh pasta?

Ravioli with Linguiça Sausage and Tomato Coulis

Lone Canary Winery | Spokane, Washington

Makes 4 small plate servings

    8 large uncooked fresh cheese-filled ravioli (about 9 ounces)

    ½ pound linguiça sausage, cut into thin slices

    Tomato Coulis (recipe follows)

    Pesto Chive Oil (recipe follows)

    4 fresh basil leaves

Bring water to a boil in a medium saucepan. Prepare the ravioli al dente according to package directions, then drain and set aside. Meanwhile, heat the linguiça sausage in a sauté pan over medium heat.

To serve, place two ravioli on the individual plates. Divide the sausage evenly and place on top of the ravioli. Top each ravioli with 1 tablespoon of the Tomato Coulis. Using a squirt bottle or a spoon, drizzle with a few lines of the Pesto Chive Oil. Garnish with a basil leaf.

Tomato Coulis

    2 medium tomatoes, blanched, peeled, and halved

    Liquid smoke, if desired

    1 ½ tablespoons extra virgin olive oil

    1 teaspoon minced garlic

    1 tablespoon diced shallot

    1 cup dry white wine

    ⅓ cup vegetable stock

    Salt and freshly ground black pepper

Preheat the oven to 200 degrees F.

Rub the cut sides of the tomatoes with a small amount of liquid smoke, if desired, and arrange them on a baking sheet. Roast the tomatoes in the oven for 1 hour, or until soft.

Meanwhile, in a medium saucepan, heat the olive oil over medium heat. Add the garlic and shallots; cook and stir until translucent, about 3 minutes. Deglaze the pan with the white wine and continue cooking until the liquid is reduced by half, about 20 minutes.

Coarsely chop the roasted tomatoes and add them to the garlic and wine mixture. Pour in the vegetable stock and simmer uncovered for 25 minutes. Using a blender or food processor, or by pressing the mixture through a food mill, purée the sauce. Strain using a mesh strainer. Season to taste with salt and pepper.

COOK'S NOTE: To blanch a tomato, bring a small saucepan of water to a boil over medium-high heat. Simmer the tomato for 2 to 3 minutes until the skin starts to tear. Remove with a slotted spoon and let cool until easy to handle. Core the tomato and slip its skin off with a paring knife or your bare hands.

Pesto Chive Oil

¼ cup prepared pesto (store-bought or homemade)

½ bunch chives, chopped

½ cup extra virgin olive oil

Pulse the pesto and chives in a food processor until thoroughly mixed. Slowly drizzle in the olive oil until a pourable consistency is achieved. Transfer the mixture into a squirt bottle.

RECIPE CONTRIBUTED BY CAPEAR CATERING

WINE PAIRING: *Lone Canary Sangiovese*

On the palate, this Super-Tuscan shows flavors of cherry, berry, and plum, finishing with fruit and tannins. Its bright acidity makes it a natural pairing with most any tomato-based pasta dish.

LONE CANARY WINERY

Despite being the state's second-largest city, Spokane has long been considered a backwater of the Washington wine industry. In recent years the wine scene has grown in Spokane and northern Idaho, creating a stronger destination. Through the years of this development, Mike Conway has quietly toiled away in Spokane. In 1993 he launched Caterina, a winery in a downtown brick building. For years he ran the operation as general manager and winemaker. In late 2002, Conway left the Caterina to launch his own operation with partners Steve and Jeanne Schaub. They named it Lone Canary in honor of Washington's official state bird, the American Goldfinch, also known as the wild canary.

The early releases, from Washington's hot 2003 vintage, were well received by critics and consumers alike, as Conway focused on a variety of red blends that were surprisingly affordable. His focus remains on red wines, as he now successfully crafts Barbera, Cabernet Sauvignon, Merlot, Sangiovese, and a couple of blends. He also makes a Rosé as well as a lone white, Sauvignon Blanc. In a Spokane wine scene that is growing crowded as well as extremely competitive, Lone Canary is standing out as a producer that stays at a very high level of quality, while keeping prices relatively modest.

Flatbread with Caramelized Onions and Butternut Squash

Camaraderie Cellars | Port Angeles, Washington

Makes 6 small plate servings

> ½ cup dried cranberries
>
> ½ cup Camaraderie Cellars Syrah or other dry red wine
>
> 1 butternut squash, peeled and cut into 1-inch cubes
>
> 4 tablespoons extra virgin olive oil, divided
>
> Salt and freshly ground black pepper
>
> 2 medium yellow onions, cut into thin slices
>
> One 12-inch flatbread or premade pizza crust
>
> 4 to 6 ounces goat cheese (chèvre), to taste
>
> ½ to 1 tablespoon finely chopped fresh rosemary, to taste

Preheat the oven to 350 degrees F.

In a small bowl, soak the cranberries in the wine for 30 minutes or until plump. Drain and set aside.

In a baking pan, toss the butternut squash with 2 tablespoons of the olive oil and season to taste with salt and pepper. Place the squash on the center rack in the oven and roast for 20 to 30 minutes, or until tender. Remove the squash from the oven and set aside.

Increase the oven temperature to 400 degrees F.

In a medium sauté pan, heat the remaining olive oil over medium heat. Add the onions; cook and stir until they are golden brown, about 20 minutes.

Place the flatbread on a baking sheet. Spread the onions on the flatbread. Top with the butternut squash, cranberries, and goat cheese. Sprinkle with rosemary. Bake for 15 to 20 minutes, or until golden and crispy. Serve immediately.

RECIPE CONTRIBUTED BY STEVE CORSON

....

WINE PAIRING: *Camaraderie Cellars Syrah*

This 100 percent Syrah is terroir driven with minerality, freshness, acidity, and deep peppery fruit flavors. A juicy example of what Syrah can be in the state of Washington.

CAMARADERIE CELLARS

You cannot get much farther away from the grapes than Don Corson does. His winery in the hills above Port Angeles, Washington, is a half-day drive to the vineyards of Eastern Washington, and the stark difference between the lush green of the Olympic Peninsula and the shrub steppe of the Columbia Valley could not be greater. Yet based on the final product, Corson would seem to be one with the vines. The red wines that come out of Camaraderie Cellars are refined and elegant, much like the man making them.

Corson and his wife, Vicki, began making wine as a hobby in the early 1980s. They turned it into their profession in 1992 and have been slowly building their business and fan base since. This boutique producer manages to acquire fruit from some of the state's top vineyards, including Champoux in the Horse Heaven Hills, Clifton on the Wahluke Slope, and Artz on Red Mountain. Corson focuses on Bordeaux-style reds, with his greatest effort a blend called Grâce (which rhymes with "floss"), a Cabernet-heavy wine that includes Merlot, Cabernet Franc, Malbec, and Petit Verdot.

A visit to Camaraderie will take you to one of the most beautiful regions of the nation—and the wine will make the trip well worth the effort. Can't make it to the Olympic Peninsula? Fortunately, Camaraderie wines are also poured at The Tasting Room in the Pike Place Market in downtown Seattle.

Buffalo-Style Flatbread Pizza

Desert Wind Winery | Prosser, Washington

Makes 7 flatbreads

¼ ounce active dry yeast

2 cups warm water, divided

5 cups all-purpose flour, divided

2 tablespoons vegetable oil

1 tablespoon salt

Buffalo Cream Sauce (recipe follows)

4 cups shredded Monterey Jack cheese, divided

2⅓ cups diced cooked chicken

14 slices bacon, cooked and crumbled

2 large green apples, peeled, cored, and diced

Whisk together the yeast and 1 cup of the warm water in the mixing bowl of an upright electric mixer until yeast is dissolved. Let mixture proof for 5 to 10 minutes. In a separate bowl, stir together the remaining water and 1 cup of the flour until a thick batter forms. Add this batter, along with the remaining flour and the oil and salt to the yeast and water mixture. Using dough hook, mix on low for 3 to 5 minutes, or until completely incorporated.

Remove the dough from the mixer and place on floured surface. Knead for 5 minutes, or until dough is slightly spongy. Put the dough in a large bowl, cover with plastic wrap, and allow to rise at room temperature for 20 to 30 minutes.

Preheat a griddle or grill to high heat.

To form the flatbread pizzas, separate the dough into seven equal portions. On a floured surface, roll the dough balls into approximately 6-inch rounds.

Cook the dough rounds 1 to 2 minutes on each side until lightly browned (flatbreads do not need to be completely cooked through, as they will be finished in the oven after they are topped).

Preheat the oven to 400 degrees F.

Arrange the cooked flatbreads on two baking sheets, cooking in two batches. Spread 2 tablespoons of the Buffalo Cream Sauce evenly over each flatbread. Sprinkle with ¼ cup of the Monterey Jack cheese, ⅓ cup of the chicken, 2 tablespoons of the bacon, and ¼ cup of the apple. Top with an additional ¼ cup of the Monterey Jack cheese. Bake each batch on the center rack in the oven for 5 to 7 minutes, or until the cheese is melted and the crust is crispy.

COOK'S NOTE: Any unused dough can be frozen for up to two weeks; precooked flatbreads can be stored in the refrigerator in an airtight container for up to three days.

Buffalo Cream Sauce

> 1½ cups heavy cream
>
> ⅓ cup hot sauce (such as Franks Red Hot Buffalo Wings Sauce)

Heat the heavy cream and hot sauce in a medium saucepan over medium heat until the sauce reduces by a quarter, about 10 to 15 minutes.

RECIPE CONTRIBUTED BY EXECUTIVE CHEF ERIC CARDENAS

....

WINE PAIRING: *Desert Wind Ruah*
Ruah, a full-bodied Bordeaux-inspired blend, is fruit-centric with just enough oak to create a spicy, toasty finish. Concentrated blackberry fruit with a hint of anise on the palate. This wine can be enjoyed with an array of foods or by itself.

DESERT WIND WINERY

For many years, Duck Pond Cellars in Dundee, Oregon, released wines from Oregon and Washington grapes. Its owners, the members of the Fries family, own one of the larger vineyards on the remote Wahluke Slope, known as Desert Wind Vineyards. So in recent years when the family opened a second facility in the Yakima Valley town of Prosser, they dubbed it Desert Wind Winery. Thanks to 540 acres of grapes at the base of the Saddle Mountains, Desert Wind has quickly developed into one of Washington's largest family-owned wineries. In 2006 the family began work on a tasting room next to the production facility. It opened in 2007 and is perhaps the most forward-thinking operation in the Pacific Northwest. In addition to the spacious and elegant tasting room, Desert Wind also has a full commercial kitchen that features lunches and dinners in season and an impressive indoor/outdoor convention facility with seating for hundreds. Upstairs are four fabulous guest rooms that overlook the Yakima River. They are a combination of the Northwest's relaxed atmosphere and European decadence.

Desert Wind's wines have the distinct advantage of starting with grapes from one of Washington's best, yet least-recognized, growing regions. They are skillfully crafted and cover a wide range of reds and whites. The flagship wine is a Bordeaux-style red blend called Ruah.

Spicy Chicken Pita

Lake Crest Winery | Oroville, Washington

Makes 4 small plate servings

   2 large pita breads

   4 ounces grilled chicken, cut into strips

   ½ cup shredded Pepper Jack cheese (about 2 ounces)

   2 peperoncinis, stemmed, cut open lengthwise, and seeded

   Spicy Sauce (recipe follows)

Warm the pita bread in the microwave for a few seconds to soften. Spread one side of the pita with a generous amount of Spicy Sauce. Put half of the chicken on one half of pita and top with half of the Pepper Jack cheese and a peperoncini. Fold in half and grill the pita using a portable electric grill on medium heat until the cheese is melted and the bread is crusty, about 4 to 5 minutes. Repeat with the second pita and cut in half to serve.

Spicy Sauce

   ¼ cup mayonnaise

   ¼ teaspoon hot pepper sauce

   Dash of seasoned salt

   1 tablespoon sun-dried tomatoes, drained and chopped

In a small bowl, mix together the mayonnaise, hot pepper sauce, seasoned salt, and sun-dried tomatoes. Cover and refrigerate until ready to use.

WINE PAIRING: *Lake Crest Sauvignon Blanc*
Clean and loaded with citrus, this wine is excellent with anything spicy. Beautiful aromas are of grapefruit and tart green apples.

Ginger Mussels

Greenbank Cellars | Whidbey Island, Washington

Makes 2 small plate servings

    2 dozen mussels, washed and debearded

    ½ cup sake

    ¼ cup plus 1 tablespoon peanut oil, divided

    ¼ cup seasoned rice vinegar

    2 tablespoons soy sauce

    1 tablespoon sesame oil

    1 cup chopped scallions

    1 to 2 jalapeño peppers, seeded and chopped

    One 1-inch piece fresh gingerroot, peeled and chopped
    (about 1 to 2 tablespoons)

    5 cloves garlic, minced

    2 teaspoons freshly ground black pepper

Put the mussels in a stainless-steel saucepan large enough to easily fit them. Pour in the sake, ¼ cup of the peanut oil, rice vinegar, soy sauce, and sesame oil. Stir in the scallions, jalapeño, ginger, garlic, and pepper. Cover the pot tightly and cook over medium-high heat until the mussels open, 5 to 6 minutes.

Remove the pan from heat and swirl the mussels in the cooking sauce. Discard any mussels that did not open.

Divide among two serving bowls. Garnish with cilantro if desired. Serve with French bread for dipping in the sauce.

. . . .

WINE PAIRING: *Greenbank Cellars Madeline Angevine*
This Alsatian-style wine has a slight floral nose and a spicy taste, with passion fruit and papaya overtones. Enjoy this white wine by itself or with seafood.

Seared Beef Tenderloin and Stilton Tartines

Windy Point Vineyards | Wapato, Washington

Makes 2 small plate servings

> 6 ounces beef tenderloin
>
> 1 teaspoon ground cumin
>
> 1 teaspoon granulated garlic powder
>
> 1 teaspoon sea salt
>
> 1 teaspoon freshly ground black pepper
>
> 2 teaspoons extra virgin olive oil
>
> ¼ cup Windy Point Estate Syrah or other dry red wine
>
> 4 thick slices of rosemary or artisan-style bread
>
> 1 clove garlic, halved
>
> 3 ounces Stilton cheese or other mild blue cheese, thinly sliced
>
> 1 cup baby arugula, washed and patted dry
>
> ½ tablespoon prepared balsamic vinaigrette (store-bought or homemade)

Remove the beef tenderloin from the refrigerator 30 minutes before preparing the dish.

Preheat the oven to 350 degrees F.

In a small bowl, mix together the cumin, garlic powder, sea salt, and pepper. Rub the spice mixture over the tenderloin. Heat the olive oil over medium-high heat in a heavy skillet. Sear the tenderloin for 2 to 3 minutes on each side. Turn the heat to low; add the Syrah to deglaze the skillet. Cover tightly with a lid to steam the tenderloin and finish the cooking, 5 to 6 minutes for medium rare. Cut the tenderloin into ½-inch-thick pieces and set aside.

Put the rosemary bread on a baking sheet and toast on the center rack in the oven for 8 minutes, or until light golden brown. Remove from the oven and rub the toast with the garlic.

Place the Stilton on the toast slices and top with a piece of tenderloin. Bake for 4 to 5 minutes on the center rack in the oven to warm the tartine. In a small bowl, toss the baby arugula with the balsamic vinaigrette and place a small mound on top of the tenderloin.

RECIPE CONTRIBUTED BY CHEF "BIG JOHN" CAUDILL

WINE PAIRING: *Windy Point Estate Syrah*
A big, rich Syrah with loads of fruit, leather, and tobacco flavors that blend perfectly and culminate in a long finish. Oak-influenced and nearly absent of tannins, this wine is plush and pleasing on the palate.

Q: How much does an average oak wine barrel cost?

A: A new French oak barrel may cost nine hundred dollars or more; a new American oak barrel costs about half as much.

Manchego Polenta with Spicy Shrimp

Forgeron Cellars | Walla Walla, Washington

Makes 4 small plate servings

    4 slices bacon, diced

    1 medium yellow onion, diced

    2 cloves garlic, minced

    1 tablespoon tomato paste

    One 14.5-ounce can fire-roasted tomatoes, undrained

    1 cup chicken stock

    1 teaspoon ground cumin

    1 teaspoon ground smoked paprika

    12 ounces medium shrimp (about 30), peeled and deveined

    Salt and freshly ground black pepper

    Manchego Polenta (recipe follows)

    ½ cup chopped fresh cilantro

In a large skillet over medium heat, cook the bacon until crisp, then drain off the excess bacon drippings. Add the onion, and cook and stir for about 8 minutes, until caramelized. Add the garlic and stir for another 2 to 3 minutes.

Stir in the tomato paste, fire-roasted tomatoes, chicken stock, cumin, and smoked paprika. Bring the mixture to a boil and simmer uncovered for 20 minutes, or until the liquid has slightly thickened. Add the shrimp and cook until pink and opaque, about 3 to 4 minutes. Season to taste with salt and pepper.

To serve, spoon the shrimp mixture over the Manchego Polenta and sprinkle with cilantro.

Manchego Polenta

3 cups water

4 tablespoons butter

¾ cup coarse ground cornmeal

1 cup shredded Manchego cheese (about 4 ounces)

In a medium saucepan, bring the water and butter to a boil over medium-high heat. Gradually add the cornmeal, whisking constantly, until well blended. Return to a boil, then reduce heat to medium-low. Cook for another 12 to 14 minutes, stirring occasionally, until the cornmeal mixture pulls away from the side of pan. Stir in the Manchego cheese until melted. Serve warm.

RECIPE CONTRIBUTED BY CHEF MICHAEL RILEY

WINE PAIRING: *Forgeron Cellars Zinfandel, Columbia Valley*

This Zinfandel has flavors on the palate of cherry compote and blueberry that are followed by a long spicy finish. Aromas are intense with licorice, blackberries, cloves, and white pepper.

FORGERON CELLARS

At first approach, Marie-Eve Gilla appears to be a diminutive young woman. That impression rarely lasts long, however. The French-born Gilla is a force unto herself, winemaking with an unwavering quest for perfection. After graduating from the University of Dijon in France's Burgundy region, she came to the New World, landing in Oregon and expecting to stay for just a few months to continue learning her craft. Yet she enjoyed the freedom of making wine in the United States, a country without the restrictions of her native France. She landed at Gordon Brothers Cellars in Pasco, Washington, for her first head winemaking job.

As luck would have it, Gilla met future husband Gilles Niçault, another French ex-pat who now makes wine for Long Shadows. With the opportunity to be a part-owner, Gilla moved to the exploding wine region of Walla Walla to launch Forgeron Cellars in 2001. The winery is at the same site as an old blacksmith shop, hence the name. The winery and its wines have been an instant hit with consumers, a feat not always simple in the ever-more-crowded Walla Walla wine scene. But this is because of Gilla's exacting wine-making, as well as her ability to track down the finest grapes. Her sources include many of Washington's top vineyards, including Pepper Bridge in Walla Walla, Klipsun on Red Mountain, Alder Ridge in the Horse Heaven Hills, and Stillwater Creek in the Frenchman Hills. Expect Forgeron to continue to rise above in the growing Washington wine industry.

Pan-Seared Halibut with Quinoa and Corn Salad

Nk'Mip Cellars | Osoyoos, British Columbia

Makes 4 to 6 small plate servings

        2 cups water

        1 cup quinoa

        6 tablespoons butter, divided

        2 finely chopped shallots, divided

        ½ cup fresh corn kernels (from 1 cob)

        ¼ cup plus 2 tablespoons Quam Qwmt Chardonnay
        or other dry white wine, divided

        Juice of 1 lemon (about 3 tablespoons)

        4 tablespoons extra virgin olive oil, divided

        Salt and freshly ground black pepper

        1 cup fresh carrot juice

        2 tablespoons heavy cream

        1½ pounds halibut fillet, cut into 4 or 6 pieces

Rinse quinoa with cold water using a fine strainer. Bring 2 cups of water to a boil in a medium saucepan. Add quinoa. Return to boil, then reduce heat to low. Cover and simmer for 15 minutes or until tender. Fluff the quinoa with a fork and set aside.

Heat 1 tablespoon of the butter in a small sauté pan over medium heat. Add half of the shallots and cook and stir until transparent, about 3 minutes. Add the corn kernels and cook until tender, about 3 minutes. Deglaze the pan with ¼ cup of the wine and the lemon juice. Continue cooking until approximately 2 tablespoons of the liquid remain. Remove pan from heat and stir in the cooked quinoa. Add 2 tablespoons of the olive oil and season to taste with salt and pepper.

To prepare the carrot sauce, heat 1 tablespoon of the butter in a small sauté pan over medium heat. Add the remaining shallots and cook until transparent, about 3 minutes. Pour in the remaining wine and reduce slightly. Add the carrot juice and reduce until approximately ⅓ cup remains. Stir in the heavy cream and reduce until sauce is slightly thickened. Carefully transfer the hot mixture to a blender and process while adding the remaining 4 tablespoons of butter 1 tablespoon at a time. Season to taste with salt and pepper.

Preheat the oven to 300 degrees F.

Season the halibut pieces with salt and pepper. In a large oven-safe sauté pan, heat the remaining 2 tablespoons of olive oil over medium-high heat. Sear the halibut on both sides until golden brown. Transfer the pan to the oven and bake uncovered for 3 to 5 minutes, or until the fish flakes with a knife. Discard skin.

To serve, place the quinoa salad in the center of the plate. Place one piece of halibut on top and spoon the carrot sauce around the dish. Garnish with chopped fresh herbs (tarragon, chervil, or basil) if desired.

....

WINE PAIRING: *Nk'Mip Cellars Chardonnay Qwam Qwmt*
On the palate, fragrant Granny Smith apple and summer fruit meld with layers of fresh pineapple and melon. Toasty oak notes blend beautifully with flavors of butterscotch and vanilla bean.

> **Q:** How many bottles of wine can be bottled from one barrel?
> **A:** About 295 bottles of wine.

Lamb with Morel Mushroom Sauce and Parmesan Polenta

Wedge Mountain Winery | Peshastin, Washington

Makes 4 small plate servings

> Extra virgin olive oil, for the roasting rack
>
> 1 rack of lamb (1 ½ to 2 pounds), frenched and trimmed
>
> 1 tablespoon finely chopped fresh rosemary
>
> 1 large clove garlic, minced
>
> 1 tablespoon grated lemon zest
>
> 1 teaspoon kosher salt
>
> ½ teaspoon freshly ground black pepper
>
> Parmesan Polenta (recipe follows)
>
> Morel Mushroom Sauce (recipe follows)

Preheat the oven to 400 degrees F.

Lightly brush the roasting rack with the olive oil. Place the lamb meat side up in the roasting pan. Mix together the rosemary, garlic, lemon zest, salt, and pepper and rub into the lamb. Roast the lamb for approximately 20 minutes, or until an instant-read thermometer inserted in the thickest part reads 135 degrees F to 140 degrees F for medium-rare. Remove the lamb from the oven and cover with aluminum foil. Let rest 10 to 15 minutes.

Cut the lamb rack into single chops. Place a small mound of the Parmesan Polenta in the center of a small plate. Top with two lamb chops. Spoon the Morel Mushroom Sauce over the chops, making sure each serving gets some morels.

COOK'S NOTE: To "french" the rack means to remove the excess fat from the rib bones. You can ask your butcher to french the lamb rack.

Morel Mushroom Sauce

2 tablespoons extra virgin olive oil

1 shallot, minced

12 small morel mushrooms, fresh or dried (rehydrated)

2 cups Wedge Mountain Winery Merlot or other dry red wine

1 cup low-sodium chicken broth

¼ teaspoon dried thyme leaves

Dash of ground cayenne pepper

3 tablespoons cold butter, cut into small pieces

In a medium saucepan, heat the olive oil over medium heat. Add the shallot and morels; cook and stir for 3 minutes. Do not brown. Pour in the wine and reduce to 1 cup. Add chicken broth and reduce to 1½ cups. Stir in the thyme and cayenne pepper. Keep warm. Slowly whisk in the butter pieces just before serving.

Parmesan Polenta

4 cups water

1 teaspoon salt

1 cup coarse ground cornmeal

1 tablespoon butter or extra virgin olive oil

½ cup finely grated Parmigiano-Reggiano cheese

1 tablespoon finely chopped chives

In a medium saucepan, bring the water and salt to boil. Slowly whisk in the cornmeal until fully incorporated. Drop in the butter and stir constantly until the polenta thickens (add a small amount of water if it gets too thick). Continue to cook, stirring frequently, until the polenta pulls cleanly away from the sides of the pan. Stir in the Parmigiano-Reggiano cheese and chives just before serving.

RECIPE CONTRIBUTED BY JOANNE SALIBY

WINE PAIRING: *Wedge Mountain Merlot*

Up front, this wine delivers the fruits promised on the nose . . . berries and a hint of black cherry. Soft and supple tannins blend with flavors of cocoa and chocolate on the finish.

Q: How full should one fill a wine glass?

A: For red wines, fill to one-third capacity. For white wines, fill halfway. And for sparking wines, fill three-quarters full.

Spinach and Feta Phyllo Squares

Hestia Cellars | Woodinville, Washington

Makes 12 small plate servings

2 tablespoons Extra-virgin olive oil

2 medium yellow onions, diced

One 20-ounce package fresh spinach, washed and patted dry

1 cup crumbled feta cheese

1 cup shredded mozzarella cheese

3 tablespoons coarsely chopped fresh Italian parsley

1 teaspoon hot red pepper flakes

½ teaspoon dried thyme (or 1 ½ tablespoons coarsely chopped fresh thyme leaves)

½ teaspoon salt

¼ teaspoon freshly ground black pepper

2 eggs

1 ¼ cups whole milk

½ cup sunflower oil or canola oil

One 16-ounce package frozen phyllo dough, thawed to room temperature

Preheat the oven to 400 degrees F.

Heat the olive oil in a medium saucepan or Dutch oven over medium heat. Add the onions, stirring frequently, until translucent, about 5 minutes. Add the spinach and cook for 2 to 3 minutes, stirring frequently, until wilted. Stir in the feta, mozzarella, parsley, hot red pepper flakes, thyme, salt, and pepper. Cook for 1 to 2 minutes, or until the cheese is melted. Set aside.

In a small bowl, beat the eggs, then pour in the milk and sunflower oil. Beat the mixture for another minute. Set aside.

Grease a 9- by 13-inch oven-safe dish. Unwrap the phyllo dough from packaging. To prevent the dough from drying out, cover with wax paper and a damp dish towel while assembling. Using two phyllo sheets per side, create flaps overhanging from each of the four sides of the dish. These flaps should hang over approximately 2 to 3 inches from the edge of the dish. Using a pastry brush, brush the phyllo sheets inside the dish with 2 tablespoons of the milk-egg mixture. Create another layer of dough inside the baking dish using two phyllo sheets. Moisten with 2 tablespoons of the milk-egg mixture.

Create four more layers of dough using two sheets per layer and moisten each layer with 2 tablespoons of the milk-egg mixture. Add a fifth layer and cover it with the spinach and feta filling. Use up the remainder of the dough making layers of two sheets per layer and moistening each layer with the milk-egg mixture. When done, turn the flaps from the side into the dish and then pour the remaining milk-egg mixture on the pastry. (If you happen to run out of milk-egg mixture, use ¼ cup milk in the very last step.)

Using a paring knife, make about a dozen small but very deep incisions on the top of the pastry. This will allow juices to penetrate the lower levels you created.

Put the dish in the oven and bake for 35 to 40 minutes (during the baking, the pastry may puff up), until golden brown. Let the pastry rest 10 to 15 minutes before serving. Cut into squares and serve warm.

....

WINE PAIRING: *Hestia Cellars Syrah*
A hedonistic wine, bursting with flavors of pomegranate and cherries, along with roasted coffee, cedar, and leather on the finish. Co-fermented with 2 percent Viognier, this well-rounded wine boasts beautiful ripe fruit flavors and bright acidity.

Kahlúa Prawns
with Lemon Buerre Blanc Sauce

Balboa Winery | Walla Walla, Washington

Makes 6 small plate servings

18 large prawns (about 1½ pounds), peeled and deveined with tails intact

1½ tablespoons extra virgin olive oil

4 slices thick-cut bacon, roughly cut into small pieces

¼ cup Kahlúa

6 handfuls mixed greens, washed and patted dry

Lemon Buerre Blanc Sauce (recipe follows)

Salt and freshly ground black pepper

Place the prawns in a bowl and drizzle with the olive oil.

Cook the bacon over medium heat in a 10-inch sauté pan until crispy, about 5 to 7 minutes. Drain off bacon fat as it accumulates. Transfer the cooked bacon to a paper towel to drain.

Drain the remaining bacon drippings from the pan and put in the prawns. Cook them on one side for 2 to 3 minutes (the prawns will start to curl). Turn the shrimp and cook for another 2 minutes. Pour the Kahlúa into the pan and, using a long lighter or match, light the Kahlúa on fire to deglaze pan. Allow the flames to burn for about 1 minute. (This will cook down the sugars and alcohol and create a thicker, more flavorful sauce.)

To serve, place a handful of mixed greens on each plate. Place three prawns on each plate and sprinkle with the bacon. Drizzle with the Lemon Buerre Blanc Sauce and season to taste with salt and pepper.

Lemon Buerre Blanc Sauce

2 tablespoons Balboa Mith White or other dry white wine

½ tablespoon minced shallot

4 tablespoons butter, cut into small pieces

½ cup whole milk

1 tablespoon lemon juice

Heat the wine and shallot over medium heat in a double boiler. Reduce until the wine is nearly gone. Turn down the heat to low and begin to add the butter one piece at a time, whisking constantly.

Once the butter is incorporated, slowly pour in the milk while continuing to whisk. Stir in the lemon juice. Allow the sauce to simmer uncovered on low heat until it coats the back of a spoon. (Do not chill or let boil.) Leave the sauce in the double boiler over hot water while preparing the Kahlúa prawns.

....

WINE PAIRING: *Balboa Mith White*
This beautiful blend of Sauvignon Blanc and Sémillon has pear, grapefruit, and passion fruit on the palate, which provides this wine with great acidity and balance.

Dungeness Crab with Lemon-Sorrel Aioli

Chateau Ste. Michelle Winery | Woodinville, Washington

Makes 2 small plate servings

    ½ cup mayonnaise

    ½ tablespoon fresh lemon juice

    1 teaspoon grated lemon zest

    ½ teaspoon Dijon mustard

    Pinch of sugar

    ½ cup finely chopped fresh sorrel

    Salt and freshly ground black pepper

    One 2- to 3-pound Dungeness crab, cooked whole

To prepare the aioli, mix together the mayonnaise, lemon juice, lemon zest, Dijon mustard, and sugar in a small bowl. Stir in the chopped sorrel and season to taste with salt and pepper. Cover and refrigerate for 4 hours or overnight.

Serve the crab in the shell chilled or warm (steam for 4 to 5 minutes). Present the aioli as a dipping sauce.

....

WINE PAIRING: *Chateau Ste. Michelle Canoe Ridge Estate Chardonnay*
This Chardonnay is inherently fresh, vibrant, and elegant. It delivers fresh apple, ripe pear, and spice aromas and flavors, with a finish that is refined with light notes of spice.

CHATEAU STE. MICHELLE WINERY

This iconic producer in the Seattle suburb of Woodinville deserves its reputation as Washington's flagship winery. It is the state's oldest and most recognized winery, and it produces a number of highly acclaimed wines that are distributed nationwide. Ste. Michelle started in 1934 as two Seattle wineries—Pomerelle and National Wine Co. Through mergers and ownership changes, the winery became Ste. Michelle Vintners in the early 1970s. The label changed in 1976 to Chateau Ste. Michelle to reflect the new facility it opened in Woodinville.

Today, the winery also serves as corporate headquarters for Ste. Michelle Wine Estates, which owns wineries in Washington (including Columbia Crest, Northstar, and Snoqualmie); Oregon (Erath); and California (Stag's Leap Wine Cellars, Villa Mt. Eden, and Conn Creek).

In the 1990s, Ste. Michelle launched two international collaborations: Col Solare, a Bordeaux-style red blend with the famed Antinori family of Tuscany; and Eroica, a Riesling with Ernst Loosen of Germany. In recent years, Ste. Michelle has ramped up its production of Riesling, one of the important grapes from its early years, and now makes more than anyone in the world—and arguably some of the best.

Through its history, Chateau Ste. Michelle has led the way for the state. Today, its far-reaching distribution and marketing efforts tell the story of Washington's quality. The winery welcomes four hundred thousand visitors a year through its doors, creating a wine industry around it in Woodinville that includes more than thirty other producers.

Seared Scallops Provençal

King Estate Winery | Eugene, Oregon

Makes 2 small plate servings

⅓ cup Extra-virgin olive oil or safflower oil

1 tablespoon capers, drained and rinsed

2 Roma tomatoes, halved lengthwise

1 sprig fresh rosemary

2 cloves garlic, minced, divided

4 large sea scallops (about 1½ inches in diameter),
rinsed and patted extra-dry

Salt and freshly ground black pepper

¼ cup King Estate Signature Pinot Gris or other dry white wine

2 tablespoons cold butter

1 tablespoon chopped fresh chives

Preheat the oven to 250 degrees F.

In a small skillet, heat the olive oil over high heat. Add the capers and fry them for 2 to 3 minutes, until they get nice and crispy. Transfer the capers to a paper towel to drain. Set aside.

Pour half the olive oil from the skillet into a small baking dish; reserve the rest in the skillet. Put the tomatoes, rosemary, and half of the minced garlic in the baking dish. Cover with foil and bake for 40 minutes, just until the tomatoes lose their firmness. Keep warm.

Just before serving, season the scallops with salt and pepper. Heat the reserved oil in the skillet to medium-high. Sear the scallops for about 3 minutes on each side. Remove them from pan and keep warm.

Add the remaining garlic and cook for 1 minute. Pour in the wine and reduce by half. Slowly stir in the cold butter. When the butter is incorporated, stir in the chives.

To serve, place the warm tomatoes and scallops in the center of each plate. Drizzle with sauce and sprinkle with the reserved capers.

....

WINE PAIRING: *King Estate Signature Pinot Gris*
This wine offers lively citrus and tropical fruit flavors with kiwi and pear notes. It has balanced acid and aromas of peach, grapefruit, and orange blossom.

KING ESTATE WINERY

A handful of folks can be credited with discovering Oregon as a place to grow great wine grapes and produce world-class wines. King Estate, however, deserves the honor of bringing the story of Oregon wines to the entire country—one bottle at a time.

The winery near Eugene, Oregon, is one of the state's largest, and it certainly produces as much Pinot Gris as anyone in North America. By themselves, King Estate's wines can stand tall with many of Oregon's best. But where the winery owned by the King family (who gained fame and fortune as producers of aviation electronics) stands out is with its marvelous distribution across the country. On store shelves and restaurant wine lists in every state, King Estate wines are ambassadors for the Oregon wine industry. The winery even uses "Oregon" instead of the more difficult to pronounce "Willamette Valley" on its label to send the message to consumers.

Closer to home, King Estate also is a good steward of the land. In a state where environmentalism nearly ranks as an official religion, King Estate has converted its vast estate holdings to organic, sustainable, and salmon-safe farming. The vineyards surround the estate winery, which looks a bit like an Italian hilltown from a distance and is one of the state's more magnificent facilities. From the quality of its wines to its vineyards to its marketing prowess, King Estate is one of Oregon's most successful wineries.

Sea Stacks with Bell Pepper Sauce

Wahluke Wine Company | Mattawa, Washington

Makes 4 small plate servings

>   1 cup extra virgin olive oil, divided
>
>   4 Diver or large sea scallops (about 1 ½ inches in diameter), rinsed and patted extra-dry
>
>   1 sushi-grade ahi tuna steak (8 ounces), finely diced
>
>   2 shallots, minced
>
>   2 tablespoons capers, drained, rinsed, and minced
>
>   ½ cup fresh lemon juice, divided
>
>   Salt and freshly ground black pepper
>
>   2 medium red bell peppers, seeded and cut into 4 pieces
>
>   2 medium yellow bell peppers, seeded and cut into 4 pieces
>
>   2 heads baby frisée or curly endive, stemmed and washed
>
>   ½ pound green beans, blanched

Preheat the oven to 400 degrees F.

In a medium skillet, heat 2 tablespoons of the olive oil until it starts to smoke. Sear the scallops on each side until golden brown, about 30 seconds per side. Put seared scallops on a baking sheet and bake for 3 minutes. Remove from the oven and let cool slightly. Slice the scallops horizontally, and keep the tops and bottoms together. Set aside

In a medium bowl, gently mix together the tuna, shallots, and capers, 4 tablespoons of the lemon juice, and 4 tablespoons of the remaining olive oil. Stir the mixture until well combined. Season to taste with salt and pepper.

In a blender or a juicer, juice the red and yellow bell peppers (keep them separate to make two different oils). If using a blender, strain the pepper after blending. Add 3 tablespoons of the remaining olive oil to each purée.

In a mixing bowl, whisk the remaining olive oil and lemon juice. Toss with the frisée and green beans. Season to taste with salt and pepper.

To serve, place a quarter of the frisée and green beans in the middle of a plate. Lay the bottom half of a scallop on the salad; place a quarter of the tuna mixture on the scallop and top with the other half of the scallop. Drizzle with the red bell pepper and yellow bell pepper oils.

RECIPE CONTRIBUTED BY CHEF RUSSELL BURTON OF THE CITY CATERING COMPANY

....

WINE PAIRING: *Wahluke Wine Company Flying Fish Riesling*
On the palate, this off-dry wine is light-bodied and balanced with crisp acidity and subtle Key lime flavors. Ripe peach and apricot flavors lead to a finish that is refreshing, with a touch of spicy minerality.

Q: How many pounds of grapes does it take to produce one bottle of wine?
A: Roughly 2.4 pounds of grapes (or 600 to 800 individual grapes).

Burton Seared Ahi with Citrus Coulis

Va Piano Vineyards | Walla Walla, Washington

Makes 4 small plate servings

> 1 tablespoon rice wine vinegar
>
> 1 tablespoon fresh orange juice
>
> 2 tablespoons orange zest
>
> 2 teaspoons lime zest
>
> One ½-inch piece fresh ginger, grated (about 1 ½ teaspoons)
>
> 1 sushi-grade ahi tuna steak (about 8 ounces)
>
> 2 tablespoons canola oil or grapeseed oil, divided
>
> Salt and freshly ground black pepper
>
> 3 tablespoons toasted white sesame seeds

In a small bowl, mix together the rice wine vinegar, orange juice, orange zest, lime zest, and ginger to create the citrus coulis. Pour the coulis into a squeeze bottle and set aside.

Brush the tuna steak with 1 tablespoon of the canola oil. Season to taste with salt and pepper. Roll the tuna in the sesame seeds, covering it completely.

Heat the remaining canola oil in a cast-iron skillet or wok over high heat. Sear the tuna on both sides until the surface is light brown, approximately 1 minute per side. Remove the tuna from the pan and let rest for 5 minutes.

To serve, slice the tuna into ¼-inch slices. Fan out the slices on individual plates. Drizzle with the citrus coulis in a zigzag pattern. Serve immediately.

RECIPE CONTRIBUTED BY SHELLIE SLETTEBAK

WINE PAIRING: *Va Piano Sémillon*

This luscious wine is rich with creamy flavors of citrus, honey, and minerals, supported by a zingy acidity. Well balanced with aromas of orange peel, ripe pear, and golden delicious apples.

VA PIANO VINEYARDS

With more than a hundred wineries crowded into the Walla Walla Valley in Washington and Oregon, it is not always easy to stand out. Those who got in early were able to seal their reputation with a customer base able to afford fine wines. More recent wineries have had to work hard to get ahead. Such is the case with Va Piano Vineyards, a stunning property owned by Justin and Liz Wylie.

Justin, a fourth-generation Walla Walla resident, returned home after attending Gonzaga University and then spending a year in Italy. That time abroad inspired him to create a winery that mirrored the best of Tuscany. In 1999, he and Liz planted and built a gorgeous vineyard and winery and Justin began to make wine as a serious hobby. In 2005, Va Piano released its first wines from the ripe, vaunted 2003 vintage. The wines—Cabernet Sauvignon and Syrah—were instant hits with critics and customers, and they have been flying out the door since. The estate vineyard is twenty acres planted with Cabernet Sauvignon, Syrah, Cabernet Franc, Merlot, and Petit Verdot. About 70 percent of the grapes are used by the Wylies, with the balance being purchased by such top producers as L'Ecole No. 41, Dunham Cellars, and Saviah Cellars.

The gated vineyard and winery are reminiscent of small Italian estates (even if the wines aren't), and one gets the feeling of stepping back into a slower pace of life while at Va Piano.

Foie Gras with Rhubarb Concasse

Dobbes Family Estate | Dundee, Oregon

Makes 8 small plate servings

> 1½ pounds rhubarb, finely diced, divided
>
> 1 cup plus 3 tablespoons sugar, divided
>
> 2 tablespoons minced shallots
>
> Juice of 2 lemons (about 6 tablespoons)
>
> 1 cup chicken stock
>
> 1¼ cup Dobbes Family Estate Rogue Valley Viognier or other dry white wine, divided
>
> Salt and freshly ground black pepper
>
> 1 teaspoon cold water
>
> ½ teaspoon cornstarch
>
> 16 ounces chilled foie gras, deveined and cut into 8 slices
>
> 16 fresh chives

In a medium saucepan, mix together all but ½ cup of the rhubarb, 1 cup of the sugar, shallots, lemon juice, chicken stock, and 1 cup of the wine. Bring to a boil. Reduce to a simmer, then cook for 30 minutes until the rhubarb is tender and the liquid is reduced by half. Remove from heat and let cool slightly.

Using a food processor or a hand-held blender, purée the rhubarb mixture until it is smooth. Season to taste with salt and pepper; set aside.

To prepare the concasse, mix together the remaining sugar with the remaining ½ cup rhubarb in a small saucepan. Add the remaining wine to cover. Simmer uncovered over medium-low heat, until the rhubarb is tender. In a ramekin, stir the cold water into the cornstarch and add this to the rhubarb mixture. Bring to a gentle boil for 10 seconds, then remove from heat and set aside.

Season the foie gras with salt and pepper. Sear the foie gras in a skillet over medium-high heat for 1 to 2 minutes on each side.

To serve, spoon the rhubarb sauce in the center of each plate. Add a slice of foie gras and place a small mound of the concasse next to it. Place two chives over each foie gras.

RECIPE CONTRIBUTED BY CARRIE WONG

....

WINE PAIRING: *Dobbes Family Estate Rogue Valley Viognier*
This Viognier is seductive, full-bodied, and enticingly aromatic. Unique in its exotic and complex qualities, this is a "red wine drinker's white wine."

DOBBES FAMILY ESTATE

At one time, Joe Dobbes made more Pinot Noir than anyone else in Oregon. He was the head winemaker at Willamette Valley Vineyards and also had started his consulting business, in which he was making wines for Torii Mor and a couple of others. Today the man known as "Hollywood Joe" because of his good looks and easy nature oversees winemaking for dozens of labels owned by others as part of his consulting operation, and he also produces a stunning array of wines under three labels of his own: Wine by Joe, Jovino, and Dobbes Family Estate.

Dobbes, whose parents also own and operate a small Oregon winery, got his start in 1985 working at wineries in Germany and France. In 1987 he moved back to his native Oregon to work at Elk Cove Vineyards in the northern Willamette Valley, then Eola Hills Wine Cellars, and Hinman Vineyards. In 1996 he landed at Willamette Valley Vineyards near Salem, as head winemaker and vice president of production, until he left in 2002 to launch Wine by Joe.

In 2003 he launched Dobbes Family Estate, a high-end label that runs the gamut of Oregon grapes, from suave vineyard-designated Pinot Noirs using Willamette Valley grapes to heady Syrahs from Southern Oregon's Rogue Valley. Dobbes never lacks energy, and his fun, easy-going attitude extends to his wines. Along the way he's also become a radio personality with a wine-related show on the air in Portland.

Blueberry Braised Short Ribs with Blue Cheese Polenta Cake

Poplar Grove Winery | Penticton, British Columbia

Makes 4 small plate servings

> 2 tablespoons extra virgin olive oil
>
> 1 clove garlic, minced
>
> 1 medium sweet white onion, thinly sliced
>
> 1 cup beef stock
>
> 1 cup Poplar Grove The Legacy or other dry red wine
>
> 1 generous tablespoon chopped fresh thyme
> (or ½ tablespoon dried crushed thyme leaves)
>
> 1 generous tablespoon chopped fresh sage
> (or ½ tablespoon dried crushed sage leaves)
>
> 1 cup fresh or frozen blueberries
>
> 1 pound beef short ribs
>
> ½ teaspoon sea salt
>
> ½ teaspoon freshly ground black pepper
>
> Blue Cheese Polenta Cake (recipe follows)

Heat the olive oil in a medium skillet over medium heat. Cook the garlic for 1 or 2 minutes, stirring frequently. Add the onions and caramelize, stirring until translucent and slightly golden, about 5 minutes. Pour in the beef stock and wine and add the thyme, sage, and blueberries.

Season the short ribs with the salt and pepper and place them in a slow cooker. Pour the onion mixture over the ribs. Cover and cook on low heat for 8 hours, or until the short ribs are tender.

To serve, unmold the Blue Cheese Polenta Cake in the center of a small plate. Cut the short ribs into four pieces. Place the short ribs on top of the polenta cake. Drizzle a spoonful of the juice from the slow cooker over the ribs. If desired, garnish with crumbled blue cheese and a sprig of sage.

Blue Cheese Polenta Cake

2 tablespoons extra virgin olive oil

2 cloves garlic, minced

2 small shallots, finely chopped

1 cup cornmeal

1 ¼ cups chicken stock

4 ounces (1 cup) crumbled Poplar Grove Tiger Blue Cheese

Salt and freshly ground black pepper

Preheat the oven to 400 degrees F.

Spray four 4-inch ramekins with cooking spray. Heat the olive oil over medium heat in a medium saucepan. Add the garlic and shallot and cook until translucent, 2 to 3 minutes, stirring frequently. Add the cornmeal and chicken stock, stirring constantly until fairly firm (the mixture will pull away from the pan), 6 to 8 minutes. Stir in the blue cheese until combined, about 3 minutes. Season to taste with salt and pepper.

Spoon the polenta into the ramekins. Place them in the oven and bake for 10 minutes or until slightly crisp. Let cool slightly before serving.

RECIPE CONTRIBUTED BY THE VICTORIA RD DELI & BISTRO

....

WINE PAIRING: *Poplar Grove The Legacy*
This is a classic blend of Merlot, Cabernet Franc, Cabernet Sauvignon, and Malbec aged in French oak. This wine demonstrates wonderful integration and finesse and pairs well with roasts of beef and lamb, steaks, and chops.

New York Steak Strips with Mushrooms and Sun-Dried Tomatoes

Trouvaille Winery | Woodinville, Washington

Makes 2 small plate servings

> One 8- to 10-ounce thick-cut New York sirloin steak
>
> ½ teaspoon garlic powder
>
> ¼ teaspoon salt
>
> ⅛ teaspoon freshly ground black pepper
>
> 5 tablespoons butter, divided
>
> ¼ cup Trouvaille Cabernet Sauvignon or other dry red wine
>
> 2 cups sliced fresh cremini mushrooms (about ½ pound)
>
> 12 sun-dried tomatoes in oil, drained and sliced

Preheat the oven to 450 degrees F.

Season both sides of sirloin steak with garlic powder, salt, and pepper. Heat 2 tablespoons of the butter in a medium skillet over medium-high heat. Sear the steak for 2 to 3 minutes per side, or until brown. Remove the steak from the skillet, preserving the juices in the skillet, and place it in an oven-safe baking dish. Cover and bake until the steak is lightly pink inside, about 18 to 20 minutes for medium doneness. Let rest for 2 minutes, then slice into ¼-inch strips.

Meanwhile, pour the wine into the skillet, heat over medium heat, and reduce by half. Set aside.

In a medium sauté pan, heat the remaining butter over medium heat and stir in the mushrooms. Cover and cook for 2 minutes. Uncover and continue cooking until moisture evaporates from the mushrooms and they turn golden brown. Keep warm.

To serve, divide the mushrooms between two small plates. Lay steak strips over the mushrooms and top with the sun-dried tomatoes. Drizzle the wine reduction over the steak. If desired, garnish with fresh sprigs of Italian parsley. Serve with a warm French baguette.

....

WINE PAIRING: *Trouvaille Cabernet Sauvignon*
This wine is beautifully dense in color, with loads of dark red fruit, including blackberry, raspberry, currant, and black cherry, as well as hints of chocolate, lavender, and coffee on the finish. The fine tannins are beautifully integrated and give the wine power and structure to age.

Fusilli Pasta with Brie and Sun-Dried Tomatoes

Griffins Crossing Winery | Lake Stevens, Washington

Makes 4 small plate servings

> 2 cups uncooked fusilli pasta
>
> ⅓ cup sun-dried tomatoes in oil, drained and chopped
>
> 3 ounces Brie, St. Andres, or Cambozola cheese (bloom removed), chopped into small pieces
>
> ¼ cup pine nuts, toasted

Bring salted water to boil in a medium saucepan. Cook the fusilli pasta until al dente (follow directions on package). Drain. Put the pasta back into the hot saucepan and place on the stovetop with the heat turned off. Add the sun-dried tomatoes and Brie, stirring until the cheese melts.

To serve, spoon the pasta mixture on individual plates and sprinkle with toasted pine nuts. If desired, garnish with chopped fresh basil.

COOK'S NOTE: To toast pine nuts, heat the pine nuts in a small skillet over medium heat. Stir until golden brown, about 3 minutes.

WINE PAIRING: *Griffins Crossing Syrah*

This 100 percent Syrah has a smoky, spicy, fruit-forward flavor with notes of pepper and cranberry. The spice and pepper in the wine especially complement foods with rich, robust flavors.

Pesto-Scallop Pouches

Legoe Bay Winery | Lummi Island, Washington

Makes 4 small plate servings

> 3 tablespoons butter, melted
>
> 3 tablespoons prepared pesto (store-bought or homemade)
>
> 6 frozen phyllo sheets (from a 1-pound box), thawed
>
> 4 teaspoons Thai sweet hot pepper sauce
>
> 8 large sea scallops (about 1 ½ inches in diameter), rinsed and patted extra-dry
>
> 3 tablespoons finely grated Parmigiano-Reggiano cheese

Preheat the oven to 475 degrees F and place the oven rack approximately 6 inches from the top of the oven. Line a baking sheet with parchment paper.

Whisk together the butter and pesto until well blended. On a smooth surface or baking sheet, smooth out one sheet of phyllo dough. Lightly brush it with the butter-pesto mixture. Cover with a second sheet of phyllo and brush it lightly with the butter-pesto mixture. Repeat with a third sheet of phyllo. Using a sharp knife, cut the phyllo stack into four even pieces, cutting crosswise and then lengthwise. Repeat with the remaining three phyllo sheets to make a total of eight phyllo rectangles.

Place ½ teaspoon of the hot pepper sauce in the center of each phyllo rectangle. Place one scallop on the pepper sauce. Fold the sides up over the scallop to form a packet. Place the pouch upside down on a baking sheet. Brush the pouch one more time with the butter-pesto mixture. Put the baking sheet in the oven and bake the pouches for 9 to 10 minutes, or until golden brown. Place two pouches on each individual plate. Sprinkle pouches lightly with cheese. Garnish with a lemon slice and sprig of basil if desired. Serve immediately (diners will need a knife and fork).

WINE PAIRING: *Legoe Bay Viognier*

A lighter-style Viognier, with nice tropical aromas and a bright, clean finish. A lush, fruit forward wine with a lovely floral nose and tastes of ripe pears and tropical fruits.

Appendix 1: Wine Pairing by Varietal

WHITES

Chardonnay
Dungeness Crab with Lemon-Sorrel Aioli (page 186)

Grilled Oysters with Cranberry Salsa (page 133)

Prosciutto-Wrapped Grilled Shrimp (page 114)

Pan-Seared Halibut with Quinoa and Corn Salad (page 176)

Pesto Chicken Spirals (page 85)

Quail Mousse Canapés (page 54)

Pinto Gris
Blue Cheese and Hazelnut Crostini (page 34)

Cardwell Hill Cheese Ball (page 13)

Chèvre with Honey and Almonds (page 12)

Seared Scallops Provençal (page 188)

White Bean, Tomato, and Olive Bruschetta (page 29)

Riesling
Crab Salad Tower with Mango and Papaya (page 148)

Crostini with Caramelized Walla Walla Sweet Onions (page 32)

Egg and Caviar Pie (page 24)

Grilled Asparagus Chèvre Tartines (page 134)

Minted Crab Salad with Chilled Cucumber Water (page 146)

Prawns and Mango Salsa Cocktail (page 105)

Prosciutto-Wrapped Pear Bites (page 53)

Sea Stacks with Bell Pepper Sauce (page 190)

Rosé
Fig and Olive Tapenade (page 2)

Grilled Coconut Curry Ceviche (page 120)

Hot Artichoke Crab Dip (page 3)

Sauvignon Blanc
Chèvre and Sun-Dried Tomato Tart (page 68)

Parmesan Wafers with Prosciutto (page 44)

Rock Shrimp with Creamy Pesto Dressing (page 150)

Salmon Mousse with Parsley and Chive Pesto (page 20)

Spicy Chicken Pita (page 168)

Sémillon
Burton Seared Ahi with Citrus Coulis (page 193)

Stilted Salmon on Crackers (page 42)

Viognier
Brie Tartlets with Grape Salsa (page 64)

Crabmeat Bruschetta (page 78)

Foie Gras with Rhubarb Concasse (page 195)

Molded Salmon Pâté (page 22)

Pesto-Scallop Pouches (page 202)

Spicy Tuna Tartar on Rice Crackers (page 36)

Baked Spinach Artichoke Dip (page 4)

OTHER WHITES
Arugula and Baby Spinach Salad (page 144)

Portobello and Gorgonzola Crostini (page 76)

Dukkah (page 14)

Dungeness Crab Gazpacho (page 142)

Phyllo-Wrapped Brie (page 8).

Ginger Mussels (page 169)

Gorgonzola-Pear Tartlets (page 63)

Kahlúa Prawns with Lemon Buerre Blanc Sauce (page 184)

Pears with Blue Cheese and Walnuts (page 140)

Roasted Vegetable and Shrimp Orzo (page 156)

Squash Napoleon with Parmesan Crisp and White Peach Sauce (page 153)

Sweet and Hot Glazed Hazelnuts (page 60)

Three-Cheese Fondue (page 6)

Truffle Popcorn with Thyme and Salt (page 41)

REDS

Barbera
Grilled Asparagus with Walla Walla Sweet Spring Onions (page 110)

Cabernet Franc
Eggplant Roll-ups (page 48)

Cabernet Sauvignon
Blue Cheese Cabernet Tri-Tips with Mushrooms (page 100)

Dried Cherry and Chèvre Wontons (page 92)

Deli Ham Roll-ups (page 28)

Endive with Roquefort and Balsamic Drizzle (page 43)

Lamb Skewers with Yogurt Cucumber Dipping Sauce (page 126)

New York Steak Strips with Mushrooms and Sun-Dried Tomatoes (page 199)

Portobello Mushrooms with Green Peppercorn Sauce (page 108)

Tenderloin Bruschetta with Horseradish and Blue Cheese (page 102)

Malbec

Beggar's Purse with Spiced Ground Lamb (page 80)

Meritage

Chèvre and Mango Steak Spirals (page 50)

Sage Shortbread Crackers (page 38)

Merlot

Lamb with Morel Mushroom Sauce and Parmesan Polenta (page 179)

Stuffed Mushroom Duxelles (page 87)

Pinot Noir

Goat Cheese and Pesto Crostini (page 30)

Gorgonzola-Stuffed Figs (page 46)

Grilled Salmon with Hazelnut-Brown Butter Sauce (page 124)

Raspberry Glazed Pork Bites (page 117)

Shiitake Tapenade with Pinot Noir Reduction (page 18)

Smoked Salmon Spread (page 11)

Sangiovese

Morel Mushroom Tempura (page 90)

Ravioli with Linguiça Sausage and Tomato Coulis (page 158)

Roasted Figs with Prosciutto (page 66)

Syrah

Beef Tenderloin with Herbed Crostini (page 83)

Crater Lake Blue Cheese Spread (page 10)

Crostini with Figs and Goat Cheese (page 71)

Flatbread with Caramelized Onions and Butternut Squash (page 162)

Fusilli Pasta with Brie and Sun-Dried Tomatoes (page 201)

Herbed Lamb Chops with Syrah Reduction (page 128)

Seared Beef Tenderloin and Stilton Tartines (page 170)

Smoky Flat Iron Steak Bites with Chimichurri Sauce (page 131)

Spinach and Feta Phyllo Squares (page 182)

Zinfandel

Manchego Polenta with Spicy Shrimp (page 173)

OTHER REDS

Baba Ganoush (page 16)

Bacon-Wrapped Dates Stuffed with Goat Cheese (page 68)

Blackberry Chipotle Sockeye Salmon (page 122)

Blueberry Braised Short Ribs with Blue Cheese Polenta Cake (page 197)

Buffalo-Style Flatbread Pizza (page 164)

Crostini with Butternut Squash and Prosciutto (page 72)

Flank Steak and Cambozola Bites (page 55)

Masa with White Beans, Pancetta, and Arugula (page 112)

Moroccan Lamb Meatballs with Spiced Tomato Sauce (page 138)

Pesto Cream Cheese Spread (page 5)

Pulled Pork Lettuce Wraps (page 94)

Spicy Lamb Meatballs with Tahini Sauce (page 58)

Spot Prawn Kabobs with Black Currant Chutney (page 118)

Three-Berry Meatball Martini (page 96)

Tuscan Bruschetta (page 75)

Appendix 2: Wine and Food Pairing Guide

WHITES

Chardonnay, serve with
- Cheese and cream sauces (butter and cream love Chardonnay!)
- Rich seafood dishes containing lobster and shrimp
- Anything with toasted nuts (if the wine is oaky)
- Such cheeses as Gruyère, Emmentaler, and Port-Salut

Gewürztaminer, serve with
- Mild seafood like crab, shrimp, and scallops
- Food grilled over aromatic woods
- Strong, spiced, or peppered cheeses

Pinto Gris, serve with
- Casual, warm-weather food (think "picnic")
- Steamed shellfish: oysters, mussels, and clams

Riesling, serve with
- Gamy birds, especially goose and duck
- Rich salty meats, like ham, sausage, and prosciutto
- Egg dishes such as quiche and frittatas
- Thai or Asian food with sweet, sour, spicy, and salty flavors

Sauvignon Blanc, serve with
- Green vegetables, salads, fresh herbs
- Spicy hot dishes

- Raw oysters
- Goat cheese (chèvre)

Viognier, serve with
- Smoked foods
- Spicy, sweet sauces like mango chutney, plum sauce, fruity BBQ sauces, and anything curry
- Most cheeses

Sparkling White Wine, serve with
- Smoky, salty, or deep-fried foods (smoked salmon, smoked almonds, tempura)
- Raw foods, like ceviche, sushi, and caviar
- Latin, Asian, and Middle Eastern cuisine
- Hard (Parmesan), rich (St. Andres), and salty (feta) cheeses

REDS

Cabernet Sauvignon, serve with
- Fattier richer dishes, especially red meat
- Dishes with toasted nuts (for oaky Cabs)
- Bitter vegetables, like radicchio, eggplant, and mustard greens

Merlot, serve with
- Roasted chicken and grilled meat
- Earthy ingredients, such as fresh herbs and mushrooms
- Dishes containing dried cherries, cranberries, and raisins

Pinot Noir, serve with
- Just about anything, except super-rich, spicy, or strong-flavored dishes
- Lamb, for a classic pairing

Sangiovese, serve with
- Simple, rustic dishes using fresh herbs
- Tomato-based dishes and pasta sauces
- Cambozola and Gorgonzola cheese

Syrah, serve with
- Robust, hearty foods: stews, chili, and barbecue
- Duck and roasted wild game
- Hard aged cheeses, like Parmesan

Zinfandel, serve with
- Sweet and spicy sauces
- Flavorful grilled dishes
- Mexican food
- Chocolate desserts (more bitter than sweet)

DESSERT WINES

Late-harvest Wines, serve with
- Citrus and tropical fruit desserts
- Berry and stone-fruit desserts
- Creamy and custard desserts

Port, serve with
- Stilton
- Chocolate, coffee, and caramel desserts

Appendix 3: Contact Information for Featured Wineries

Tasting room location noted in listings with multiple addresses.

WASHINGTON

àMaurice Cellars
178 Vineyard Lane
Walla Walla, Washington 99362
509-522-5444
www.amaurice.com
The tasting room is open to the public on
Saturday or by appointment.

Bainbridge Island Vineyards and Winery
8989 Day Road E
Bainbridge Island, Washington 98110
206-842-9463
www.bainbridgevineyards.com
The tasting room is open to the public on
Friday, Saturday, and Sunday.

Balboa Winery
4169 Pepper Bridge Road
Walla Walla, Washington
509-301-6932
www.balboawinery.com
The tasting room is open to the public
by appointment only.

Benson Vineyards Estate Winery
754 Winesap Avenue
Manson, Washington 98831
509-687-0313
www.bensonvineyards.com
The tasting room is open to the public daily.

Bergevin Lane Vineyards
1215 W Poplar Street
Walla Walla, Washington 99362
509-526-4300
www.bergevinlane.com
The tasting room is open to the public daily.

Brian Carter Cellars
14419 Woodinville-Redmond Road
Woodinville, Washington 98072
425-806-WINE
www.briancartercellars.com

The tasting room is open to the public
Thursday through Monday.

Camaraderie Cellars
334 Benson Road
Port Angeles, Washington 98363
360-417-3564
www.camaraderiecellars.com
The tasting room is open to the public Friday,
Saturday, and Sunday (May through September), special weekends, or by appointment.

Canyon's Edge Winery
10 Merlot Drive
Prosser, Washington 99350
509-786-3032
www.canyonsedgewinery.com
The tasting room is open to the public daily.

Challenger Ridge Winery
3095 Challenger Road
Concrete, Washington 98237 (Winery)
14344 Woodinville Redmond Road NE
Redmond, Washington 98052 (Tasting Room)
877-396-5379
www.challengerridge.com
The winery and tasting room are open to the
public Saturday and Sunday.

Chateau Ste. Michelle
14111 NE 145th Street
Woodinville, Washington 98072
425-488-1133
www.ste-michelle.com
The tasting room is open to the public daily.

Chatter Creek Winery
18658 142nd Avenue NE
Woodinville, Washington 98072
325-485-3864
www.chattercreek.com
The tasting room is open to the public
Saturday and Sunday.

Chinook Wines
220 Wittkopf Loop
Prosser, Washington 99350
509-786-2725
www.chinookwines.com
The tasting room is open to the public
Saturday and Sunday (May through October)
or by appointment.

Covington Cellars
18580 142nd Avenue NE
Woodinville, Washington 98072
425-806-8636
www.covingtoncellars.com
The tasting room is open to the public
Friday through Sunday.

Desert Wind Winery
2250 Wine Country Road
Prosser, Washington 99350
509-786-7277
www.desertwindwinery.com
The tasting room is open to the public daily.

DiStefano Winery
12280 Woodinville Drive SE
Woodinville, Washington 98072
425-487-1648
www.distefanowinery.com
The tasting room is open to the public
Saturday, Sunday, and by appointment.

Dry Falls Cellars
6828 22nd Avenue NE
Moses Lake, Washington 98837
509-762-5922
www.dryfallscellars.com
The tasting room is open to the public
Saturday, Sunday, and by appointment.

Edmonds Winery
19501 144th Avenue NE D-500
Woodinville, Washington 98072
425-774-8959

www.edmondswinery.com
The tasting room is open to the public
Saturday and Sunday

Fielding Hills Winery
1401 Fielding Hills Drive
East Wenatchee, Washington 98802
509-884-2221
www.fieldinghills.com
The tasting room is available
by appointment only.

Flying Trout Wines
37 S Palouse Street
Walla Walla, Washington 99362
509-520-7701
www.flyingtroutwines.com
The tasting room is open to the public on
Saturday (closed February through April).

Forgeron Cellars
33 W Birch Street
Walla Walla, Washington 99362
509-522-9463
www.forgeroncellars.com
The tasting room is open to the public daily.

Gamache Vintners
505 Cabernet Court
Prosser, Washington 99350
509-786-7800
www.gamachevintners.com
The tasting room is open to the public daily.

Gård Vintners
19495 144th Avenue NE, Suite B240
Woodinville, Washington 98072
509-346-2585
www.gardvintners.com
The tasting room is open to the public
Friday through Sunday, and by appointment.

Gifford Hirlinger
1450 Stateline Road
Walla Walla, Washington 99362
509-529-2075
www.giffordhirlinger.com
The tasting room is open to the public
Friday, Saturday and Sunday

Greenbank Cellars
3112 Day Road
Greenbank, Washington 98253
360-678-3964
wine@whidbey.com
The tasting room is open to the public
Thursday through Monday.

Griffins Crossing Winery
2008 123rd Street SE
Lake Stevens, Washington 98258
425-280-6845
www.griffinscrossing.com
The tasting room is open to the public on the
first Saturday and Sunday of the month.

Hedges Family Estate Winery
53511 N Sunset Road
Benton City, Washington 99320
509-588-3155
www.hedgesfamilyestate.com
The tasting room is open to the public
Friday, Saturday, and Sunday (March through
November).

Hestia Cellars
18572 142nd Avenue NE
Woodinville, Washington 98072
425-333-4270
www.hestiacellars.com
Tasting is available by appointment only.

Hightower Cellars
19418 E 583 PR NE
Benton City, Washington 99320
509-588-2867
www.hightowercellars.com
The tasting room is open on Friday
and Saturday or by appointment.

Kyra Wines
8029 Andrews Street NE
Moses Lake, Washington 98837
509-750-8875
www.kyrawines.com
The tasting room is open for special events
and by appointment. Friday through Sunday,
and by appointment.

Lake Crest Winery
2021 Highway 7 N
Oroville, Washington 98844
509-476-2347
www.lakecrestwinery.com
The tasting room is open to the public daily.

Legoe Bay Winery
4232 Legoe Bay Road
Lummi Island, Washington 98262
360-758-9959
www.legoebaywinery.com
The tasting room is open to the public—
call for hours.

Lone Canary Winery
109 S Scott Street, B2
Spokane, Washington 99202
509-534-9062
www.lonecanary.com
The tasting room is open to the public
Thursday through Sunday.

Long Shadows Vintners
1604 French Town Road
Walla Walla, Washington 99362
www.longshadows.com
509-526-0905
The tasting room is open by appointment
only.

Lost River Winery
26 Highway 20
Winthrop, Washington 98862
509-996-2888
www.lostriverwinery.com
The tasting room is open to the public Friday,
Saturday, and Mondays, or by appointment.

Maryhill Winery
9774 Highway 14
Goldendale, Washington 98620
877-627-9445
www.maryhillwinery.com
The tasting room is open to the public daily.

Mercer Estates
3100 Lee Road

Prosser, Washington 99350
509-786-2097
www.mercerwine.com
The tasting room is open to the public
Wednesday through Sunday.

North Shore Wine Cellars
221 W Steuben Street (Highway 14)
Bingen, Washington 98605
509-493-3881
www.northshorewinecellars.com
The tasting room is open to the public
everyday except Tuesday (summer);
and Friday through Monday (off-season).

Paradisos del Sol
3230 Highland Drive
Zillah, Washington 98953
509-829-9000
www.paradisosdelsol.com
The tasting room is open to the public daily.

Patit Creek Cellars
325 A Street
Walla Walla, Washington 99362
509-522-4684
www.patitcreekcellars.com
The tasting room is open to the public
everyday except Monday.

Pondera Winery
12806 NE 125th Way
Kirkland, Washington 98034
425-825-3917
www.ponderawinery.com
The tasting room is available
by appointment only.

Reininger Winery
5858 W Highway 12
Walla Walla, Washington 99362
509-522-1994
www.reiningerwinery.com
The tasting room is open to the public daily.

Robert Karl Cellars
115 W Pacific Avenue
Spokane, Washington 99201
509-363-1353

www.robertkarl.com
The tasting room is open to the public
Saturday and Sunday or by appointment.

RockWall Cellars
110 Nichols Road
Omak, Washington 98841
509-429- 5121
www.rockwallcellars.com
The tasting room is open to the public daily.

Sweet Valley Wines
7 W Poplar Street
Walla Walla, Washington 99362
509-526-0002
www.sweetvalleywines.com
The tasting room is open to the public on
Saturday and Sunday or by appointment.

Tapteil Vineyard Winery
20206 E 583 PR NE
Benton City, Washington 99320
509-588-446
www.tapteil.com
The tasting room is open to the public Friday
through Sunday (April through December) or
by appointment.

Terra Blanca Winery and Estate Vineyard
35715 N DeMoss Road
Benton City, Washington 99320
509-588-6082
www.terrablanca.com
The tasting room is open to the public daily.

Tildio Winery
70 E Wapato Lake Road
Manson, Washington 98831
509-687-8463
www.tildio.com
The tasting room is open to the public
daily (summer) and weekends (winter).

Trio Vintners
596 Piper Avenue
Walla Walla, Washington 99362
509-529-8746
www.triovintners.com

The tasting room is open to the public
Saturday and Sunday or by appointment.

Trouvaille Winery
16735 NE 139th Place
Woodinville, Washington
425-861-8020
www.trouvaillewinery.com
The tasting room is not open to the public.

Tucker Cellars Winery
70 Ray Road
Sunnyside, Washington 98944
509-837-8701
www.tuckercellars.com
The tasting room is open to the public daily.

Trust Cellars
1050 Merlot Drive
Walla Walla, Washington 99362
509-529-4511
www.trustcellars.com
The tasting room is open to the public
Thursday through Sunday (March through
December) or by appointment

Tytonidae Cellars
2580 Cottonwood Road
Walla Walla, Washington 99362
509-301-8834
www.tytonidaecellars.com
The tasting room is open by appointment
only.

Vin du Lac Winery
105 Highway 150
Chelan, Washington 98816
509-682-2882
www.vindulac.com
The tasting room is open to the public daily.

Va Piano Vineyards
1793 JB George Road
Walla Walla, Washington 99362
509-529-0900
www.vapianovineyards.com
The tasting room is open to the public Friday,
Saturday, and Sunday.

Wahluke Wine Company
23934 Road T 1 SW
Mattawa, Washington 99349
509-932-0010
www.flyingfishwine.com
The tasting room is not open to the public.

Wedge Mountain Winery
9534 Saunders Road
Peshastin, Washington 98847
509-548-7068
www.wedgemountainwinery.com
The tasting room is open to the public
Thursday through Monday.

Westport Winery
1 South Arbor Road
Aberdeen, Washington 98520
360-648-2224
www.westportwines.com
The tasting room is open to the public daily.

William Church Winery
19495 144th Avenue NE, Suite A100
Woodinville, Washington 98072
425-427-0764
www.williamchurchwinery.com
The tasting room is open to the public
Saturday and Sunday or by appointment.

Windy Point Vineyards
420 Windy Point Drive
Wapato, Washington 98951
509-877-6824
www.windypointvineyards.com
The tasting room is open to the public daily
(May through October) and Thursday through
Monday (November through April).

Woodinville Wine Cellars
17721 132nd Avenue NE
Woodinville, Washington 98072
425-481-8860
www.woodinvillewinecellars.com
The tasting room is open Saturday
or Friday by appointment only.

Yellow Hawk Cellar
343 S Second Avenue,

Walla Walla, Washington 99362
509-529-1714
www.yellowhawkcellar.com
The tasting room is open to the public
Friday through Monday.

Zefina Winery
1910 Fairview Avenue E, Suite 500
Seattle, Washington 98102
206-453-0293
www.zefina.com
The tasting room is not open to the public.

OREGON

Cardwell Hill Cellars
24241 Cardwell Hill Drive
Philomath, Oregon 97370
541-929-9463
www.cardwellhillwine.com
The tasting room is open to the public daily
(May through Thanksgiving).

Cliff Creek Cellars
128 W Main Street
Carlton, Oregon 97111
503-852-0089
www.cliffcreek.com
The tasting room is open to the public daily
(June through September) and Friday
through Monday (October through May).

Daedalus Cellars
10505 NE Red Hills Road
Dundee, Oregon 97115
503-537-0727
www.daedaluscellars.com
The tasting room is open to the public
by appointment only.

De Ponte Cellars
17545 Archery Summit Road
Dayton, Oregon 97114
503-864-3698
www.depontecellars.com
The tasting room is open to the public daily.

Devitt Winery
11412 Highway 238
Jacksonville, Oregon 97530

541-899-7511
www.devittwinery.com
The tasting room is open to the public daily.

Dobbes Family Estate
240 SE Fifth Street
Dundee, Oregon 97115
503-538-1141
www.dobbesfamilyestate.com
The tasting room is open to the public daily.

Et Fille Wines
c/o August Cellars
14000 NE Quarry Road
Newberg, Oregon 97132
503-449-5030
www.etfillewines.com
The tasting room is open by appointment
only.

King Estate Winery
80854 Territorial Road
Eugene, Oregon 97405
541-942-9874
www.kingestate.com
The tasting room is open to the public daily.

Natalie's Estate Winery
16825 NE Chehalem Drive
Newberg, Oregon 97132
503-554-9350
www.nataliesestatewinery.com
The tasting room is open to the public
Memorial Day weekend, Labor Day weekend,
Thanksgiving weekend, Valentine's Day
weekend, or by appointment.

Phelps Creek Vineyards
1850 Country Club Road
Hood River, Oregon 97031
541-386-2607
www.phelpsvineyards.com
The tasting room is open to the public
Thursday through Monday (May through
October) and Saturday and Sunday (March,
April, and November).

Rex Hill Vineyards
30835 N Highway 99W

Newberg, Oregon 97132
800-739-4455
www.rexhill.com
The tasting room is open to the public daily.

Rosella's Vineyard and Winery
184 Missouri Flat Road
Grants Pass, Oregon 97527
541-846-6372
www.rosellasvineyard.com
The tasting room is open to the public
Thursday through Monday, and Tuesday and
Wednesday by appointment only.

RoxyAnn Winery
3285 Hillcrest Road
Medford, Oregon 97504
541-776-2315
www.roxyann.com
The tasting room is open to the public daily.

Scott Paul Wines
128 S Pine Street
Carlton, Oregon 97111
503-852-7300
www.scottpaul.com
The tasting room is open to the public
Wednesday through Sunday.

Springhouse Cellar
13 Railroad Avenue (First and Cascade)
Hood River, Oregon 97031
www.springhousecellar.com
541-308-0700
The tasting room is open to the public
Friday through Sunday (Memorial Day
through Labor Day) or by appointment

The Four Graces
9605 NE Fox Farm Road
Dundee, Oregon 97115
503-554-8000
www.thefourgraces.com
The tasting room is open to the public daily.

Torii Mor Winery
18325 NE Fairview Drive
Dundee, Oregon 97115
503-538-2279; 800-839-5004

www.toriimorwinery.com
The tasting room is open to the public daily.

Trium Winery
7112 Rapp Lane
Talent, Oregon 97540
541-535-6093
www.triumwine.com
The tasting room is open to the public
Friday, Saturday, and Sunday (May through
September) or by appointment.

Troon Vineyard
1475 Kubli Road
Grants Pass, Oregon 97527
541-846-9900, ext. 113
www.troonvineyard.com
The tasting room is open to the public daily.

Vista Hills Vineyard
6475 Hilltop Lane
Dayton, Oregon 97114
503-864-3200
www.vistahillsvineyard.com
The tasting room is open to the public daily.

Weisinger's of Ashland
3150 Siskiyou Boulevard
Ashland, Oregon 97520
541-488-598; 800-551-WINE
www.weisingers.com
The tasting room is open to the public daily
(May through September) and Wednesday
through Sunday (October through April).

Wheatridge in the Nook Winery
11102 Philippi Canyon Road
Arlington, Oregon 97812
541-454-2600
www.wheatridgeinthenook.com
The tasting room is open to the public daily.

Winter's Hill Vineyard
6451 Hilltop Lane
Lafayette, Oregon 97127
503-864-4538
www.wintershillwine.com
The tasting room is open to the public daily

(May through October) and weekends
(December through April) or by appointment.

Winderlea Vineyard & Winery
8905 NE Worden Hill Road
Dundee, Oregon 97115
503-554-5900
www.winderlea.com
The tasting room is open to the public Friday,
Saturday, and Sunday (Memorial Day through
Thanksgiving).

Wooldridge Creek Vineyard and Winery
818 Slagle Creek Road
Grants Pass, Oregon 97527
541-846-6364
www.wcwinery.com
The tasting room is open to the public
by appointment only.

BRITISH COLUMBIA

Black Widow Winery
1630 Naramata Road
Penticton, British Columbia
V2A 8T7 Canada
250-487-2347
www.blackwidowwinery.com
The tasting room is open to the public most
Saturdays (summer and fall).

Bounty Cellars
#7-364 Lougheed Road
Kelowna, British Columbia
V1X 7R8 Canada
250-765-9200
www.bountycellars.com
The tasting room is open to the public
Monday through Friday or by appointment.

Elephant Island Orchard Wines
2730 Aikins Loop
RR1 S5 C18
Naramata, British Columbia
V0H 1N0 Canada
250-496-5522
www.elephantislandwine.com
The tasting room is open to the public daily
(April through November), or by appointment.

House of Rose Winery
2270 Garner Road
Kelowna, British Columbia
V1P 1E2 Canada
250-765-0802
www.houseofrose.ca
The tasting room is open to the public daily.

Mission Hill Family Estate
1730 Mission Hill Road
Westbank, Okanagan, British Columbia
V4T 2E4 Canada
250-768-6448
www.missionhillwinery.com
The tasting room open is to the public daily

Nk'Mip Cellars
1400 Rancher Creek Road
Osoyoos, British Columbia
V0H 1V0 Canada
250-495-2985
www.nkmipcellars.com
The tasting room is open to the public daily.

Paradise Ranch Wines
#901-525 Seymour Street
Vancouver, British Columbia
V6B 3H7 Canada
604-683-6040
www.icewines.com
The tasting room is not open to the public.

Poplar Grove Winery
1060 Poplar Grove Road
Penticton, British Columbia
V2A 8T6 Canada
250-493-9463
www.poplargrove.ca
The tasting room is open to the public daily
(June through October) and weekends (May).

Salt Spring Vineyards
151 Lee Road
Salt Spring Island, British Columbia
V8K 2A5 Canada
250-653-9463
www.saltspringvineyards.com
The tasting room is open to the public daily
(summer) and Saturdays throughout the year
(except January).

See Ya Later Ranch
2575 Green Lake Road
Okanagan–Similkameen D, British Columbia
V0H 1R0 Canada
250-497-8267
www.sylranch.com
The tasting room is open to the public daily
(April through October).

Sumac Ridge Estate Winery
17403 Highway 97 N
Summerland, British Columbia
V0H 1Z0 Canada
250-494-0451
www.sumacridge.com
The tasting room is open to the public daily.

Tinhorn Creek Vineyards
32830 Tinhorn Creek Road
Oliver, British Columbia
V0H 1T0 Canada
250-498-3743
www.tinhorn.com
The tasting room is open to the public daily.

Index

About the Author

Catherine Handfelt

Carol Frieberg has pursued her passion for healthful living in the food and wellness field for twenty-five years. She is a former food editor for General Mills where she served as spokesperson for Betty Crocker. Carol has authored five cookbooks, including *Breakfast in Bed* and *The Best Places to Kiss Cookbook*, and has made numerous media appearances on television, radio, and in print.

Carol is currently a health educator and weight-loss coach, dedicated to helping people improve the quality of their lives through better health and nutrition. She enjoys sharing her enthusiasm for healthy foods that are simply prepared, and develops recipes out of her home test kitchen. Carol lives in Seattle where she enjoys visiting farmers markets and local wineries and exploring the bountiful Pacific Northwest.

Winery profiles written by Andy Perdue, founder and editor-in-chief of *Wine Press Northwest* and the author of *The Northwest Wine Guide: A Buyer's Handbook.*